EAN SEIGNEVR DE CREQVI .

Bruges 1429.

155

322.

Le Roy De Pologne

MESSIRE GVY DE
PONTAILLER. SEIG. DE
Talmer. A Dijon 1433.

324

Le Comte de CHAROLOIS · 1433 ·

CONTENTS

HERALDRY
ITS ORIGINS AND MEANING

Michel Pastoureau

Heraldry is the science that studies armorial bearings, the coloured emblems pertaining to an individual, a family or a community. Their composition is governed by the specific rules of blazon that distinguish the medieval European heraldic system from all other systems of emblems, whether earlier or later, military or civil.

CHAPTER 1
HISTORY OF ARMS

The first arms, which appeared on battlefields and at tournaments, were made to be seen from a distance. Bright and contrasting colours and very stylized devices helped to identify the bearer. Opposite: the poet-knight Hartmann von Aue. Right: the leader of the papal knights.

The use of arms

Heraldry remains a misunderstood science; it is wrongly regarded as esoteric and has sometimes been given a poor reception by the general public. One of the main reasons for these reactions is that membership of the gentry or nobility and bearing arms have often been seen as being synonymous with each other. On the continent of Europe, the use of armorial bearings has never been restricted to a particular social class at any time between the 12th (when they first appeared) and the 20th centuries. Every individual, every family, every group and community has been free to adopt the arms of their choice and to put them to any private use they please, provided they have not wrongfully assumed the arms of another. The few restrictions relate solely to the public use of arms and to a few heraldic accessories (coronets, mantles, insignia of rank) that may accompany modern shields. The position in England is quite different. Only gentlemen are qualified to bear arms.

Although everyone on the continent of Europe has the right to bear arms, not everyone necessarily does. Especially in very early times, arms were used more

Arms were often displayed at tournaments, but also at festivals and carnivals, such as the one held at Nuremberg at the end of the 15th century. Rich butchers played an important part in them.

frequently by some social classes and groups than by others: the nobility, the aristocracy, higher-ranking magistrates and merchants, rich artisans. They were rather like the modern business card: anyone can have one but not everyone does.

The arms of commoners bore a far wider variety of charges than the arms of the nobility. They also tended to include a larger number of plants and everyday objects (furniture, clothes) and, in particular, tools.

Origins: neither classical nor eastern

From the end of the Middle Ages, treatises on heraldry put forward several hypotheses to try and explain its origins. Over the centuries, the number of explanations continued to increase. Father Claude-François Ménestrier lists some twenty of them in his work *Le Véritable art du blason et l'origine des armoiries*, published in 1671. Some fanciful theories, such as those that attribute the invention of arms to Adam,

Noah, Alexander, Julius Caesar or King Arthur, were rejected early on, generally towards the end of the 16th century. Others, based on more serious arguments, survived longer but were gradually refuted by the work of late 19th- and early 20th-century heraldists.

Today the three theories that were for a long time favoured by heraldists have been abandoned. The first – dear to medieval and 16th-century writers – held that the first 12th-century arms continued the tradition of military or family emblems used in classical Greece and Rome. The second theory, long preferred by German heraldists, proposed that runes, barbarian insignia and Germano-Scandinavian emblems of the first millennium had a dominant influence on the development of feudal heraldry. Last and most important, for it was given credence for the longest time, was the theory that heraldry originated in the East and that the West took over a Muslim (or Byzantine) custom during the first Crusade.

Today experts agree that the appearance of arms in western Europe has nothing to do with the Crusades, or the East, or the barbarian invasions, or ancient Rome, but that it is linked, firstly, to

In feudal times, shields were decorated with ornamental devices, some of which, several decades later, became genuine heraldic charges. That is the case with the trellis decoration seen on this chesspiece dating from the end of the 11th century.

the transformation of feudal society after the year 1000 and, secondly, to the development of military equipment between the end of the 11th century and the first decades of the 12th century: arms did not exist at the time of the first Crusade; they were well established by the time of the second.

They first appeared in the West, where the right conditions existed; it is in the West that we must seek the reasons for their appearance.

The combatants shown on Greek vases (below) sometimes bear shields representing animal figures (eagles, lions, griffins) that more or less resemble those on medieval arms. Sometimes they are purely decorative devices, sometimes the attributes of protective divinities, sometimes

Arms on the battlefields

Between these two periods, western combatants, who had been unrecognizable because of the hood of their coat of mail (which nearly reached chin level) and the nosepiece of their helmet (which covered their face),

insignia alluding to the user's name. But there is no link between these ancient Greek emblems and heraldic charges.

For a long time heraldists believed that the earliest documented arms were those of Geoffrey Plantagenet, Count of Anjou and Duke of Normandy, who died in 1151. On his enamelled funeral plaque, formerly in Le Mans Cathedral, he is shown holding a huge azure shield strewn with golden lions (left). A chronicler from Anjou tells that on his marriage in 1127 Geoffrey received from his father-in-law, Henry I, a shield strewn with lions. Unfortunately this text was written towards 1175, in fact nearly twenty-five years after the death of Geoffrey, and the funerary plaque was created around 1155–60, at the request of his widow Matilda. So Geoffrey Plantagenet probably never bore arms. Moreover, it has yet to be established which are the oldest extant arms, although that is a rather futile exercise. The appearance of arms is not due to any individual initiative but was a social phenomenon that took place over a fairly long period of time, between approximately 1120 and 1150.

gradually adopted the custom of having devices depicted on the large expanse of their almond-shaped shield as a means of identification in battle and, even more often, in the early tournaments. These devices were geometrical, animal or floral, and were painted in bright colours. They became genuine armorial shields when they were constantly used by the same person and the composition obeyed certain simple, fixed and recurrent conventions. This custom became established in the first half of the 12th century. Subsequently, genuine professionals of wars and tournaments, the heralds of arms, endeavoured to transform these practices into rules and to copy the arms borne by the combatants in compilations they used as *aides-mémoires*: 'rolls of arms'.

However, the origins of heraldry cannot merely be explained in terms of the development of military equipment. The appearance of arms is more deeply rooted in the new social order that took shape in western society in the feudal period. Like the patronymic names that appeared during the same period, or the iconographical attributes that were becoming increasingly common, heraldry gave a

The Bayeux tapestry tells of the conquest of England by the Norman duke, William the Conqueror. It was completed around 1080, that is two generations before the appearance of arms. In fact, the devices decorating the shields of the tapestry – the crosses, saltires and dragons – are not real heraldic charges. The same individual is represented in several places bearing different arms. Nevertheless, this tapestry is an important pre-heraldic document because, in one scene showing the Battle of Hastings, William is seen raising his helmet to show his soldiers that he is not dead (detail above). This action is clear proof that it became necessary to use signs as a means of identification in the heat of battle.

new identity to a society that was reorganizing itself. It helped to situate individuals within groups and these groups within the social system as a whole. For that reason, arms, which were originally individual emblems, became hereditary from the end of the 12th century and acquired their definitive form as a result of being passed down through the same family.

The spread of arms throughout society

Used at first by princes, barons and lords, arms were gradually adopted by the entire western aristocracy. By the early 13th century, about 1500 distinct coats were in use in England. At the same time, they spread to non-combatants, to commoners and to various corporate bodies: one by one, women (from 1180, sometimes earlier), the clergy (towards 1200), patricians and bourgeois (towards 1220), artisans (towards 1230), towns (from the end of the 12th century), corporations (towards 1240), civil and religious communities (late 13th and early 14th centuries) adopted arms. In some regions (Normandy, Flanders) even peasants sometimes bore arms. As for the Church itself, although at first it distrusted a system that had evolved entirely outside its sphere of influence – as attested by the use, from the outset, of the vernacular language in describing arms – it

Dukes and counts adopted arms before the kings did. France does not in fact seem to have chosen the famous shield of Azure semy of Fleurs-de-lis Or as its arms until rather late. The earliest document is on a shield, not that of King Philip Augustus himself but that of his son, who became Louis VII (reigned 1137–80); it is appended to a charter, dating from 1211 (left). The first coloured representation of these Capetian arms occurs several years later on a stained-glass window in Chartres Cathedral. The kings of France certainly did not have a monopoly on the fleur-de-lis. It is a common heraldic charge, found on many seals; for example, in the early 13th century it appears on the seal of a viscount of Thouars (above).

fully supported the use of arms from the 14th century on. Henceforth, ecclesiastic monuments became real 'museums' of armorial bearings. Arms were found on the floors, the walls, the windows and the ceilings and on devotional objects and vestments. They also played a considerable role in the religious art of the late Middle Ages and the Baroque period.

It was largely thanks to seals that the use of arms spread to non-combatants. Very soon the lords and knights were not satisfied with having the arms they had adopted painted on their shields. They also had them depicted on their banners, horse trappings, tunics, and on various items of moveable and immoveable property they owned, especially on their seals, symbol of their legal personality.

Seals extended the use of arms to women (below, the seal of Eleanor of Castile, wife of Edward I) and to corporate bodies (left), such as the seal of the town of Damme in Belgium. In the 13th century, most written documents were sealed – an unsealed document was in fact regarded as suspect, and each of the contracting parties or witnesses committed himself by his seal. Some two thirds of seals are based iconographically on arms or heraldic devices inscribed directly on the field.

In France, the 16th-century wars of religion, followed by the ravages of the revolutionary period, destroyed a large number of the arms displayed in churches. In neighbouring countries, however, they remained very common, even in Protestant ones, since the war against images did not extend to these secular representations of arms. Church windows, in particular, offer the heraldist considerable information on the late Middle Ages and the early modern period. Opposite: arms in Bristol Cathedral. Left: a stained-glass window at Bere Regis Church, Dorset. Below right: a representation of Jean du Mez, Marshal of France, wearing a surcoat of arms, on a window of Chartres Cathedral. However, church windows prove very difficult to date, identify or authenticate. Moreover, they are often situated at a great distance from the viewer. Many stained-glass windows, whether armorial or not, were not designed to be observed closely; they act as important decorative features.

From genuine arms to imaginary arms

Gradually everyone who possessed a seal acquired the habit of filling its field with arms, as the aristocracy did. In western Europe about a million medieval armorial bearings are in existence; of these, three quarters are known from seals and a good third of them are not noble arms.

Arms did not originate in one well-defined place. They appeared at the same time in various regions of western Europe: the countries between the Loire and

Throughout the 13th and 14th centuries, everyday objects were 'heraldized'. This Swiss wooden coffer covered with painted parchment is a good example from the early 14th century.

the Rhine, England, Switzerland, northern Italy. Later they spread from these centres. By the early 14th century this new fashion extended throughout the West and even began to reach the Christian East.

As the use of arms spread geographically and socially, so more and more objects, fabrics, garments, works of art and monuments were covered with arms; they fulfilled a triple function as signs of identity, marks of command or ownership and ornamental motifs. They became such a common feature of social life, attitudes and culture that even by the end of the 12th century arms were sometimes attributed to imaginary persons (heroes of novels, legendary figures, mythological creatures) and to famous men from classical antiquity and the late Middle Ages, who had clearly never borne arms.

New forms of emblem

As the 18th century approached, so more and more arms were borne by private individuals and corporate bodies throughout Europe. Some ten million European armorial bearings have been published or identified covering the period from the 16th to the late 18th centuries.

In the late Middle Ages, armorial bearings were very closely linked to both life and death. The tombs (opposite, the tomb of Philippe Pot, Great Chamberlain of Louis XI) display not only the arms of the deceased but also those of their ancestors. Similarly, clothing could be decorated with wedding arms. The Countess of Salisbury (above, chained to her husband in memory of the indissoluble bond of marriage) wears a long cloak that combines the arms of her husband with those of her father.

Ⓜore often, perhaps, than in wars, in which few real battles took place, it was in tournaments that the 12th-century knights tended to use the unchanging and codified heraldic marks as a means of identification. Tournaments remained, until the mid-16th century, the main forum for heraldic rituals in aristocratic circles. Standard treatises, such as the one written by King René of Anjou in the mid-15th century (left and overleaf), describe the procedure. A tournament generally lasted three days and opposed two teams (it was only in jousting that knights fought one against one). It was preceded by the presentation of arms, banners and crests, which enabled the spectators, ladies and heralds of arms – who ensured respect for the rules of chivalry – to identify the participants and applaud their feats.

The decline in the use of the seal, which was replaced by a signature or the intervention of a notary to authenticate documents, was not mirrored by a decline in the use of arms. In fact, on the continent of Europe, arms were placed on a wide variety of objects, subject to virtually no control and governed solely by the rules of blazon (a written description of heraldic arms). However, in England the use of arms was monitored closely by heralds during their Visitations or tours of inspection around the country.

Baroque art even infused arms with new vigour, especially in Italy, Austria and southern Germany. And it was indeed in these regions that the use of arms spread in society, probably reaching its peak towards the mid-17th century. From the mid-18th century their use declined in France, faced with increasing competition from new forms of emblem: ciphers, monograms, badges, liveries, devices.

The abundance of arms in modern Europe does

From the end of the Middle Ages onwards, arms were supplemented or rivalled by insignia of office or rank, badges, collars, devices, ciphers, monograms (opposite, 17th-century manuscript listing the emblems of the various guilds in the city of Orvieto). Some designs fused these different formulas, such as this majolica plate displaying

not make it easy to record or even count them at all exhaustively. All attempts to do so have failed in face of the principle that on the Continent everyone is free to adopt and use

the arms of Pope Julius II surmounted by the papal insignia: tiara and keys; or the arms of Death in a woodcut by Albrecht Dürer (left).

On maps and charts (above, a planisphere dating from 1573), the arms not only identify the kingdoms, provinces and cities but also show how the new worlds were divided up between the various European powers.

arms. It is that principle that has enabled heraldry to survive through the centuries, to adapt to many systems – including the Communist regime, which endowed many of its sovkhozy and kolkhozy (state-owned and collective farms) with arms – and to resist most of the social and cultural changes that transformed Europe between the 12th and the 20th centuries. A separate place must be given to the attempt to record arms that was made in France in the late 17th century.

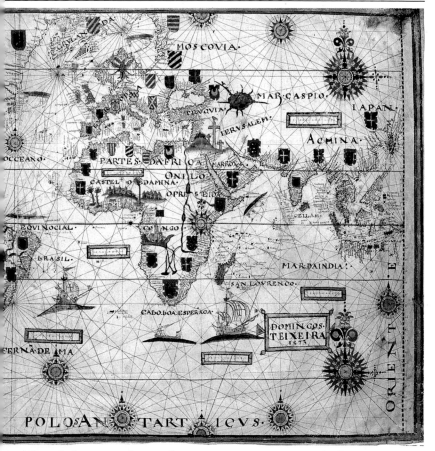

The 1696 *Armorial général*

In November 1696 a royal edict was promulgated in France ordering all arms borne in the kingdom to be listed so that they could be recorded in a huge collection: the *Armorial général*. This edict was certainly not intended to restrict the bearing of arms to specific social classes, as has sometimes been alleged. Quite the contrary, it set out to record all arms borne in the kingdom in the hope that there

The playing cards designed in the 17th century are a useful source of information on heraldry, genealogy and geography. The same engravers and merchants supplied the public with playing cards and geographical maps.

E D I T

D U R O Y,

would be a large number. The real intention of the edict was to increase tax revenues: it was one means, among others, of pouring money into the state coffers that had been emptied by the wars of the League of Augsburg against France in 1686. On pain of a fine of 300 francs and the confiscation of their armorial property, all those who bore arms – noblemen and commoners, individuals and communities – had to have them registered and to pay a tax for this. The tax varied depending on the status of the owner; it was twenty francs – a large sum – for private individuals. Those who subsequently wanted to alter their arms had to have them re-registered and pay the tax again.

Despite repeated threats of fines and confiscations throughout the year 1697, not many arms were registered. That is why it was decided by a decree of the king's council on 3 December 1697 to create in every administration and district 'rolls' on which would be inscribed the names of all individuals and communities considered to be armigers. After the publication of the rolls, they would have a week to register their arms – and pay the registration charge – failing which they would be officially assigned arms. Many individuals – magistrates, doctors, merchants, artisans, clerks – and communities who had never borne arms and had no intention of doing so were forced to adopt them or, more often, officially given them. It was for them that Charles d'Hozier, who was in charge of the *Armorial*, and his clerks created series of similar shields, based on simple variations on the same tinctures (any of the colours or metals used on

Armorial bindings (below, a binding from the 1580s with the arms of the great bibliophile Jacques-Auguste de Thou) can be found on medieval manuscripts. They proliferated in the 16th and 17th centuries, but were then supplemented or replaced by the heraldic bookplate, now positioned inside the book. Both are an invaluable source of information on modern heraldry.

ion d'une Grande Maiſtriſe Generale
& établiſſement d'un Armorial Ge-
Depoſt public des Armes & Blaſons
& création de pluſieurs Maiſtriſes
ans les Provinces.

Le Corps des marchands Bonnetiers de cette Ville de Paris.

La Communauté des Chirurgiens.

La Communauté des trente Jurez Crieurs de la Ville et Fauxbourgs de Paris.

La Communauté des Jurez Mouleurs de Bois de la Ville de Paris.

N. . . . Chomas, md bourg de paris.

Having one's name and arms registered in the *Armorial général* of 1696 was by no means a proof of nobility (left, a page from the *Armorial* showing the arms of Parisian corporations). Only one sixth of the hundred and twenty thousand or so arms listed belong to nobles or noble families. But the general public is often unaware of this. In their frantic search for blue blood, people continue to believe that, if they can only discover an ancestor – or even the same surname! – in this immense compilation, they will be able to prove their noble ancestry. Certain rather unscrupulous dealers actually try to encourage this illusion.

heraldic arms) or charges (a pictorial representation depicted on heraldic arms) in a given town or region.

That was also the time when a number of 'canting arms' were created, those where the charge is a pun on the owner's name, or rather ridiculous 'allusive arms', which were diligently recorded in the *Armorial général* but obviously never used by their recipients. Thus a Breton apothecary was assigned a shield charged with a syringe and three chamber pots, while a Norman lawyer, answering to the name Le Marié (the married man), was endowed with a shield decorated with a pair of horns!

The French Revolution at war with arms

In France, the mistake of equating arms with the nobility mainly dates from the French Revolution. In its famous session of 19 June 1790, the Constituent Assembly decreed the suppression of arms at the same time as that of the nobility, titles, liveries, banners, pennons, orders of chivalry, decorations and all the 'signs of feudalism'. The use of arms was

UNITE.
ET
INDIVISIBILITE
DE LA
RÉPUBLIQUE
LIBERTÉ,
ÉGALITÉ,
FRATERNITÉ
OU LA MORT

It was on the suggestion of Viscount Mathieu de Montmorency (left) that the Constituent Assembly added arms to the list of 'signs of feudalism' to be suppressed by decree.

abolished. But if the Constituent Assembly had taken the trouble to look around, it would have found that arms were in no way marks of nobility, even less signs of feudalism: many commoners and artisans bore them, as did most towns, institutions and communities. In 1790 more than two thirds of arms in use in the kingdom of France were not borne by nobles and a good third of them were borne by corporate bodies. But the damage had been done, and even though they were restored under the Empire and then the Restoration, arms never regained the place they had in the Middle Ages under the *ancien régime*. Hence, the fairly wide difference today between France, where heraldry is a science that looks mainly at the past, and most of its neighbouring countries, where it has remained much more alive by renovating the signs and visual codes that form part of daily life. The Constituent Assembly's decree was ratified by the letters patent of Louis XVI dated 22 June. It gave rise to a real hunt for coats of arms. In 1791 and 1792 several successive decrees ordered the destruction of arms on moveable and immoveable property, both public and private, and fixed the penalties – always very severe – to be imposed on those who continued to use them. The only exception made was for objects 'relating to the arts', which were not to be mutilated but taken to the nearest museum or depot. Individuals had to 'cancel' or burn their titles, scrape the arms off their crockery

The French Revolution soon had to construct a new system of emblems and symbols. However, it did not do so by creating much that was new but drew largely on the existing range, such as the arms of the freemasons and those that appeared during the War of American Independence. After the establishment of the republic in 1792, a range of emblems was created but none of them really managed to supplant the earlier ones. Only the cock (opposite), which had

in fact been seriously compromised under the *ancien régime* (above, Louis XVI), remained a national figure, watching over its native land and heralding the advent of a new era.

Left: report by the inspector of highways on undestroyed arms in 1790.

Le soussigné Inspecteur de Voierie a remarqué, rue .... dans petits champs No a l'hotel du controle general que l'on a pas supprimés les armes qui existe au dessus de la porte cochere du d. hotel.

Baillou

or silver, tear up the bindings of their books, turn over their fire-backs, hammer down the lintels of their doors. After the fall of the monarchy, on 21 September 1792, this hunt spread to the ancient attributes of royalty, especially crowns and fleurs-de-lis. For several months a kind of collective madness fired the hunt for these. In August 1793 the spire of the Sainte Chapelle in Paris was knocked down because it was partially decorated with L (for Louis) and fleurs-de-lis.

From the First Empire to the present day

This 'heraldic terror' did not cease until 1796. Napoleon restored arms in 1808, soon after creating an imperial nobility to whom he wanted to reserve their use. To this end, the heraldists of the First Empire devised an ingenious

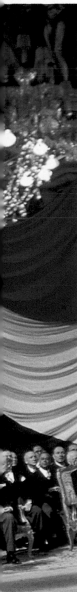

system of blazon that exactly described the rank and function of every armiger. This system, more theoretical than aesthetic (since the arms were heavily charged) and virtually inapplicable, did not have time to enter into force. In 1814 Louis XVIII put an end to the heraldic fancies of the First Empire. As in the Middle Ages and under the *ancien régime*, all noblemen or commoners, individual or corporate bodies were once again free to adopt and use the arms of their choice, to use them privately at will, to change them whenever they fancied, provided – as ever – they did not wrongfully assume the arms of another.

That is still the principle that prevails today in most European countries. Only monarchies where the nobility has a real legal status (such as the United Kingdom, Belgium, Netherlands) have official bodies that can register, protect or control arms. In the United Kingdom, the College of Arms, founded in 1484, is the official registry of arms for England,

The United Kingdom remains the country in which heraldry has left the strongest imprint on institutions and the monarchy. The Office of Garter King of Arms has existed since 1415. Garter is the principal King of Arms and is usually styled Garter Principal King of Arms. The Office of Norroy King of Arms has existed since the late 13th century and that of Clarenceux King of Arms since c. 1334. The Earl Marshal (the Duke of Norfolk) presides over state ceremonial and is assisted by the heralds. The royal arms of England (centre) occupy the place of honour below the Union Jack.

Napoleon Bonaparte chose the eagle, imperial figure *par excellence*, as the emblem of his empire (far left).

Wales and other countries of which the Crown is Sovereign, with the exception of Scotland, and, since 1988, Canada, which established a heraldic authority in that year. The power and jurisdiction to consider and resolve heraldic problems is vested in England in The High Court of Chivalry.

Elsewhere total freedom prevails, including the freedom not to respect the rules of blazon. Signs, devices and emblems of all kinds, in particular logos, flourish and occur on the sidelines of heraldry, with which they

Gabon (below, its flag) uses arms similar to the European ones. Only the animal figures are borrowed from local fauna.

There are many varied examples of heraldry in contemporary insignia and emblems. The former USSR, for example, has always made immoderate use of very strong visual signs, often inspired by the principles of heraldry, to advertise its regime (left) and its ideology (opposite, a march past on Red Square in 1985).

sometimes compete. Some cities, businesses and communities have abandoned their traditional arms in favour of a logo. Others have retained their arms but have often augmented them with an emblem regarded as more modern. The use of arms by private individuals is frequent in Scandinavia, Scotland and Switzerland, but less common in England, Germany and central Europe and rare in France and southern Europe. Since the 18th century, the bearing of arms has spread far beyond Europe, first towards the Christian New World, then to Asia, Africa and Oceania. This internationalization of European heraldry, which has become more marked in recent decades, has often been to the detriment of indigenous systems of emblems, some of them centuries old. All the black African countries, for instance, use European-style flags and arms instead of their own tribal or ancestral emblems.

Although some large European cities have abandoned the traditional arms that sometimes date back to the Middle Ages in favour of entirely new and not very imaginative logos – the initial of the city's name, for example – others have managed to combine both formulas: they have adopted the main charge on their arms as their logo (below, the city of Paris). In this way they do not turn their back on either the past or the present.

Heraldry is both a social code and a system of signs. This system is based on charges and tinctures that are arranged on the shields according to certain conventions, principles and rules. The body of these rules and of the repertoire of charges and tinctures forms a type of grammar that is called blazon.

CHAPTER 2

THE LANGUAGE OF HERALDRY

With its six basic tinctures, open choice of devices and endless possible combinations of arms, blazon is a very flexible code that has come down through the centuries and adapted to social change. Opposite: folio from a French armorial. Left and right: two English arms.

Precise rules, strict composition

Armorial bearings are made up of two elements, charges and tinctures, which are placed on a shield whose contour lines can take various shapes. The triangular form, inherited from medieval shields, is not obligatory, it is simply the most common. Some arms are inscribed in a circle, an oval, a square, a lozenge (frequently so in the case of women's arms from the 16th century in England) and there are even countless arms whose border is in fact the same as that of the object on which they are placed. If this object is a banner, the trappings of a horse or a piece of clothing, its border may also form the border of the arms.

Within the shield, tinctures and charges cannot be used or combined at will. They obey a small number of binding rules of composition. These are the rules that most clearly distinguish European arms from types of emblem used by other cultures.

On the peasant arms of the Germanic countries we find a variety of linear symbols (opposite above); they were also used as marks of ownership on objects and buildings. We find similar symbols in other societies, especially in the form of cattle brands (left, camel brands from the Sahara).

In Asia, Africa, pre-Columbian America and the Muslim states we may therefore find, at any one time, emblems that more or less closely resemble western arms, though they are never composed on the basis of a code of strict, unchanging rules.

The six tinctures of heraldry

The main rules of blazon relate to the use of tincture. This generic term covers both metals – Or (gold/yellow) and Argent (silver/white) – and colours – Gules (red), Azure (blue), Sable (black) and Vert (green).

The first five can be found everywhere and are very common on the arms of all periods and all regions. The sixth, Vert, is less common, for reasons that have never been fully explained. There is also a seventh tincture, found even less frequently: Purpure (purple), not really regarded as a real heraldic tincture

The circular design frequently seen in Japan (above) is more rare in Europe; yet European arms were sometimes inscribed on elaborately shaped shields. A shield (opposite) from Burgundy.

These heraldic tinctures are absolute, conceptual, almost immaterial: the tones do not matter. For instance Gules can be vermilion, cerise, carmine, garnet red, etc.; what counts is the idea of red and not the material and chromatic representation of that tincture. The same applies to Azure, Sable and Vert, and even to Or and Argent, which can be rendered by yellow and white (as is commonly the case) or by gold and silver. For instance, on the arms of the King of France, Azure semy of Fleurs-de-lis Or, the Azure can be sky blue or ultramarine and the fleurs-de-lis lemon yellow, orange yellow or gold, it really does not matter. The artist is free to translate Azure and Or as he sees fit, depending on the material he is working on, the techniques he is using and his own aesthetic sense. In the course of time the same arms can therefore be represented in very different tones.

The rules of blazon

Blazon arranges its six tinctures in two main groups – metals and colours. (There is also a third group, furs: Ermine and Vair.) It places Argent and Or in the first, Gules, Sable, Azure and Vert in the second. The basic rule is that a colour may not be placed on a colour or a metal on a metal. To take the case of a shield depicting a lion: if the field of this shield is Gules (red), the lion may be Argent (silver/white), Or (gold/yellow) but not Azure (blue), Sable (black) or Vert (green) because Azure, Sable and Vert belong to the same

group as Gules.
Conversely, if the field of the shield is Argent, the lion can be Gules, Azure, Sable or Vert, but not Or. These fundamental rules have existed since the origin of arms and have almost always been respected – it is rare to find one per cent of infringements in a given body of arms. It is assumed that this rule was borrowed from banners and their

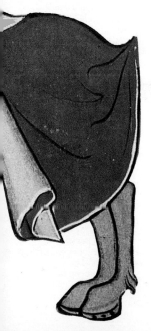

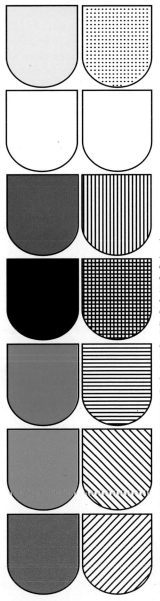

Arms without charges and consisting of a single tincture are rare. In blazon they are described as 'plain'. A spectacular example from the *Manesse Codex*, a famous Zurich manuscript of the early 14th century that reproduced the poems of more than 130 German-speaking troubadours, is shown opposite: it depicts an unknown poet-knight (*der Dürner*) bearing 'Gules plain' arms.

In the late 15th century, the spread of black-and-white engraved and printed images led to the disappearance of an essential feature of armorial representation: tincture. For some decades designers therefore endeavoured to hand-colour arms on woodcuts, in imitation of illuminated manuscripts. Then, in the 16th century, different systems of letters and signs were designed to replace the heraldic tinctures. But this did not prove very satisfactory. Finally, in the early 17th century, engravers in Antwerp perfected a simple system of hatching to designate the seven heraldic tinctures, which was gradually adopted by all the typographical workshops.

insignia, which had a considerable influence on early arms, and was primarily a question of visibility. The first arms, which all had two tinctures, were designed as visual signs made to be seen from afar and immediately identifiable in battle. In fact red is easier to distinguish when placed against white or yellow than against blue, black or green.

But these questions of visibility do not fully explain these rules. They also date back to the very rich symbolism of tinctures during the feudal period, a symbolism that was undergoing major changes at the time. For the new social order that was becoming established in the West after the millennium was accompanied by a new system of tinctures: white, red and black were no longer the only basic tinctures as was often the case in classical antiquity and the late Middle Ages; blue, green and yellow were now promoted to the same rank, in social life as in all the codes relating to it. The emergent science of heraldry was one of these codes.

Whatever their origin, over the centuries these rules on the use of tinctures governed all the arms that were created. However, they were often infringed when two or more different arms were combined (or marshalled) within one shield and two tinctures that should in principle not touch each other necessarily became adjacent. When Edward III proclaimed himself King of France in 1337, he combined the

The binding rules on associating blazon tinctures were not confined to arms. They soon spread to most of the designs on flags, especially banners, military insignia and ships' ensigns. That is why modern flags, which have often inherited these insignia, are also based on the seven basic tinctures

4

(with orange replacing purple) and generally respect the heraldic rules of tincture association. Today, more than eighty per cent of the two hundred or so national flags used in the world remain faithful to this rule. Below and above: the flags of France (2), Poland (3), Iceland (4), Sweden (5), Finland (6) and Hungary (7).

The wheel is a motif that is rarely found in heraldry. The most famous example is that of the Archbishop of Mayence (above). Opposite top right: wheels on a shield in a 17th-century armorial.

1

2   **3**

arms of the two kingdoms on the same shield. In the new shield created by 'quartering', the Azure field of the arms of France necessarily touched the Gules field of the arms of England.

The charges: an unlimited choice

Tinctures make up the essential component of arms. For although arms without charges do exist, there are none without tinctures, even though some arms are only known to us through monochrome documents,

5   6   7

such as seals or coins. But the range of charges that can be displayed on them is obviously much wider. It is unlimited: any animal, plant, object or geometrical form can become a heraldic charge. Over the centuries, new devices continually widened the range of choice. In our century, for example, several cities that have airports display stylized aeroplanes on their arms, while some winter sports resorts depict two Skis in saltire. Similarly, in the former USSR and Romania under Communist rule, several kolkhozy or collective farms were attributed arms decorated with combine harvesters or other agricultural machines. In these cases we are far away from the heraldic spirit.

For film-producers and their public, arms still evoke the Middle Ages, hence the need to display them on the shields of knights in films inspired by medieval days. Below: a scene from Eric Rohmer's *Percival the Gaul* (1978).

For although anything can be a heraldic charge, not everything is. The range of charges normally used was in fact fairly small, at least until the 17th century. During the decades following the appearance of arms in the 12th century, it was confined to some twenty charges. Subsequently, the number continued to grow; but until the end of the Middle Ages not more than forty or so charges were in use. The range of choice became more diversified in the 17th and 18th centuries in particular, first in the Germanic countries and central Europe, then outside Europe, when other continents began to turn to heraldry: exotic plants and animals started to appear on shields.

For a long time it was fairly rare to find plants, except for the fleur-de-lis and rose, and everyday objects on arms. The charges encountered most frequently consisted, in almost equal proportions, of animals, geometrical figures (or ordinaries) resulting from the division of the shield into a certain number of bands or compartments, and small charges that were also more or less geometrical but could be placed anywhere on the shield: bezants, annulets, lozenges, stars, billets and so on. At the end of the Middle Ages and at the beginning of the modern age, when the range became more diversified, it was primarily plants (trees, flowers, fruit, vegetables) and

Some of the geometrical designs encountered on arms are based on the structure of genuine shields used in the 11th and 12th centuries (they were made of a number of wooden ribs held together by a metal frame), others on the structure of feudal banners (made from pieces of differently coloured fabric stitched together). They could be based on straight lines, but also on engrailed, wavy, bendy, broken, embattled or more or less indented lines or take the form of crosses, flames or plumes. An infinite number of variations was possible. The range of arms adopted by individuals and corporate bodies grew over the centuries and it was partly this variety of linear forms that prevented arms looking too similar.

The *Manesse Codex* depicts several poet-knights in full heraldic dress. Some bear arms charged with devices that are unusual or difficult to identify, which is why this splendid manuscript was described in the 17th century as a 'fantastic' armorial. Left: the arms of Wolfram von Eschenbach, author of the famous *Parzival* which inspired Wagner, charged with two axes addorsed or back to back.

The plough is a rare heraldic charge that is difficult to represent schematically. However, like other agricultural machines, it is found on the arms of former kolkhozy under the Communist regime. The arms of the kolkhoz of Vnorovy in former Czechoslovakia (above) depict the whole plough realistically. In the Middle Ages, only the ploughshare would have been shown, in a highly stylized manner.

Some heraldic charges may look rather incongruous, such as this turnip in a Swiss 16th-century stained-glass window representing the Virgin Mary, Jesus and St Peter. But the owner of these arms, who no doubt paid for the window, was proud to be represented and to show his family arms as they were. They help identify him, just as the two keys symbolize St Peter.

objects (arms, tools, clothes) that were added to the original charges. After that shields were charged with buildings, parts of the human body, letters of the alphabet and even actual scenes, which turned some arms into small pictures that were illegible and contrary to the spirit of heraldry.

As the range of charges on which people could draw to create arms diversified over the centuries, so

the number of charges placed on each shield increased. In the 12th and 13th centuries, there were generally only two charges per shield; in the 18th century it was quite common to place four, five, six or even more different charges on a shield, which was therefore divided up into several compartments.

Over the generations the main charge was joined by several secondary ones. Family arms rarely stayed exactly the same; they often tended to become more complex with time, especially among the nobility.

The eagle versus the lion

From the outset, animal figures were an essential and original component of heraldry. On a

The only heavenly body to appear frequently is the star. From the 17th century it in fact became the second most common heraldic charge, a close second to the lion. The sun and the moon appear less often and are sometimes given a human face, as in these arms of the heavens in a 16th-century treatise on blazon (above) or the arms of the painter Jacob Grün, a member of the brotherhood of St Christopher of Arlberg, and his wife (left).

This breast from which a few drops of milk are dripping is an exceptional charge, seen only on the arms of the English family of Peter Dodge of Stopford (left). It underlines the way heraldry and humour often coexisted happily.

blanckene · Giriéboirch

balkenstein · helfenstein

zayn · eppenstein · Rechinstein · diefstein

beebarde · h̃ya hasenfin · der Scenk v̄ erbach · blinckenberch

Brenendorch · eyst · ħ bepdmū ūā Weynsberch · ħ ħedenc ūā wildenb

ħ Gherijnt vā weynsberch · ħ hedenc vā wildenb

The Bellenville Armorial

This armorial derives its name from one of its early owners, Antoine de Beaulaincourt, lord of Bellenville, King of Arms of the Order of the Golden Fleece, who died in 1559. It is one of the most beautiful painted armorials from the Middle Ages. The design is confident and precise, the charges stylized, the colours bright and luminous. Compiled in the second half of the 14th century, this armorial shows more than 1300 armorial bearings from throughout Europe, classified by 'marches of arms', that is according to a system that is both feudal and geographical. On these pages are the arms of the Archbishop of Trier (opposite) and of the Archbishop of Cologne (left), together with the arms of their respective vassals. The armorial also includes four hundred arms of participants in jousts and tournaments, military campaigns and expeditions to Prussia, where noblemen throughout the West went to help the Teutonic knights fight the Russians, Poles and Lithuanians.

nassou Limburgen

Spanem Spanem Spanem

ysenborch croneborch

biborch artborch gryborch wirtheym

knnebel petborch lienenstein die coppen

frystan groufen kamerer ondenem

Opposite page, left to right from the top to the second from bottom row:

1. Azure semy of Billets a Lion rampant Or
2. Untinctured *(for Azure)* three Eagles displayed Argent
3. Checky Or and Azure
4. Checky Argent and Gules
5. Gules a Wheel Argent
6. Argent two Bars Sable
7. Quarterly Gules and Vair in the first quarter a Crown Or
8. Gules a Bend between two Lions passant bendwise Or
9. Gules three voided Cinquefoils Or
10. Or an Eagle displayed Gules a Bordure Vair
11. Azure three Cinquefoils Argent voided Or On a Chief also Or an Eagle displayed issuant Sable
12. Argent an Inescutcheon Gules and in dexter chief an Annulet Purpure
13. Per pale Or and Gules over all a Fess Vert and in dexter chief an Anchor reversed Purpure
14. Or three Lozenges conjoined in fess Sable

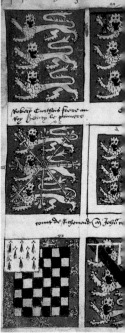

third of all arms, the main charge is an animal. The lion is certainly the most popular heraldic charge in every region, period and social class. Nearly fifteen per cent of European arms are charged with a lion – a little more in the Middle Ages, a little less in modern times. That is a considerable proportion, since the next charges in order of frequency, the 'Fess' and the 'Bend', that is two geometrical designs or 'ordinaries', account for less than five per cent. In fact, when arms became established in the course of the 12th century, the lion became the definitive king of the beasts in all the western traditions. Previously, the bear had been king in much of Germanic, Celtic and Scandinavian Europe.

The heraldic lion is always shown in profile, more often erect (rampant) than lying down (couchant). In early English armory, until the late 14th century, any lion that was not rampant was called a 'Lion leopardé'. This term may date back to an ancient Greek convention that distinguished between the lion, usually shown with a heavy mane and in profile, and the leopard, which had less hair and was shown

The eagle is the only bird or beast frequently shown with two heads (left). This charge is fairly rare in the Middle Ages and not well explained. It would seem that heraldry borrowed the motif from eastern fabrics, which were in turn the legacy of an early graphic tradition. The most famous double-headed eagle is the one on the arms of the Holy Roman Empire, whose form was determined under the reign of Emperor Sigismund in the early 15th century.

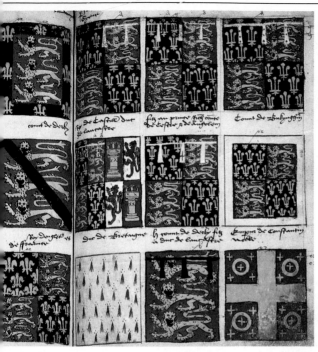

The arms of England (left, the arms of the King and his family from an early 16th-century English armorial) were created under the reign of Richard the Lionheart (1189–99). In 1195, after his return from captivity, he transformed the shield with two facing lions 'rampant' that he had borne until then – and which his father, Henry II Plantagenet (reigned 1154–89), may also have borne – into a shield with three lions 'passant guardant' (first line of document above), which all his successors retained and which later acquired the name 'leopards' on the Continent. The reasons for this change have not yet been fully explained. In fact, the heraldic leopard is simply a variant of the lion. Opposite above: four lion shields from an English Ordinary of Arms, that is one that classifies arms by charges and not by owners, from the early 15th century. If the leopard had not been shown facing the spectator but in profile, it would have simply been a lion 'passant'.

looking towards the observer. Later the term leopard was applied only to the 'Lion passant guardant', that is a lion walking, with its right forepaw raised and its head facing the spectator, as in the royal arms of England; hence the expression 'the leopards of England'. Nowadays, the term leopard applies only to the real animal, which is rarely found in blazon.

After the lion comes the eagle, king of the skies and sometimes competing with the lion for the throne of king of the beasts – in modern times, in fact, empires have all chosen the eagle and not the lion as their heraldic emblem. In heraldry, the two animals are more or less mutually exclusive: in regions where lions are frequently displayed (Belgium, Luxembourg, Denmark, for instance) there are few eagles, and vice versa (Austria, northern Italy). The blazoned eagle is also rather unlike the real

animal. It is shown flattened, its body facing the spectator and its head in profile, with a very prominent beak and claws. The eagle appears on about two per cent of European arms, especially those of the nobility.

From the real to the fantastic: the heraldic bestiary

Other animals occur less frequently and form a bestiary that has not changed for a long time. The stag or hart and the boar, the game the aristocracy most liked to hunt, appear from the beginning, as do the bear and the wolf. The wolf is most common in Spanish heraldry. Domestic animals are more rare, appear later and are less common among the nobility. Dogs – recognizable by their collar – and cattle tend to be found more on peasants' arms in some countries on the Continent, while sheep can be displayed on the arms of towns and religious communities. The horse occurs in English heraldry, though on the Continent it is notable for its absence. Sometimes considered as a mere tool, sometimes as the equal of humans, it had a status of its own in early societies.

Apart from the eagle, the main birds represented on shields are the raven, the coot, the swan, a certain number of waders (cranes, herons, storks) and a few ducks, peacocks, ostriches and parrots. The dove and the pelican are found mainly on ecclesiastical arms. As for the falcon, it is as rare as the horse, although it was the bird medieval aristocracy preferred. But the bird most commonly seen on

For a long time the bear remained the king of the beasts in northern European tradition. This role was taken over by the lion in the 12th century. But, even at that time, defeating a bear in single combat was a great achievement and the victor would proudly display a bear's head on his arms. Perhaps that is what one of the ancestors of the poet Hawart von Holzwang did (opposite), while Wachsmut von Künzingen (above) was content with a pair of peaceful fish.

European arms is not real at all; archetypal and stylized, it cannot be identified as belonging to a particular species. The heraldic term for it is the martlet, although it has little to do with the martin. It is a small bird, always shown in profile and generally repeated several times on the same shield. It was represented without feet from the end of the 13th century and in France it was deprived of its beak from the Renaissance. As used in heraldry, this bird looks more like a small geometrical device (star, bezant, lozenge) than an animal; it is often shown on arms in England, northern France and the Netherlands.

Much the same applies to a fish known as the pike (or luce). It bears little resemblance to a real pike and is a stereotype fish, with an elongated body; generally two fish are represented upright and back to back on the shield. The pike is the charge most often borrowed from the fish world. Equally stylized but

On Germanic arms, there is a greater variety of blazoned fauna than in England and France. At the end of the Middle Ages these animals were depicted in inventive and fanciful forms. This was a forerunner of Baroque heraldry and it is quite common to find surprising compositions in which animal figures are associated with features normally alien to them. One example is this wolf (above) wearing a doublet on the canting arms of the Bavarian Wölflin family depicted on an early 16th-century tombstone.

I t is unusual to find insects on arms. When they do appear, they are almost always canting charges.
Left: the arms of the Waldbiene family (in German *Biene* means bee) on a tombstone in a 15th-century Tyrolean church.

A mong the rarest fabulous beasts are the unicorn, recognizable by its cloven feet and the large horn on its forehead, the griffin, half eagle, half lion, and the dragon, whose form continually changes and is made up of different parts. Below: animal arms from the armorial of Konrad Grünenberg dating from the late 15th century.

more curvilinear and with an enormous head and a kind of crop is the dolphin, which again bears little resemblance to the cetacean of the same name.

Lastly, it should be noted that monsters, hybrid creatures (sirens, chimeras) and fabulous beasts (unicorns, dragons, griffins) are much more rare on arms than is generally believed. They only entered the bestiary and mythology of heraldry at a late date and in limited numbers.

The design and composition of coats of arms

The first arms had a simple design: a device of one tincture placed on a field of a different tincture. Since the arms were meant to be visible from afar, the design was schematic and any features that would help identify them were stressed or exaggerated: the contours of geometrical forms, the head, feet or tail of animals, the leaves and fruit of trees. The device occupied the entire field of the shield and the two tinctures, bright and clear, were associated according to the rules described earlier. These few principles, born on battlefields and at tournaments, formed the basis of the heraldic style, which every designer had to follow in order to remain faithful to the original spirit of heraldry.

Over the centuries, however, armorial bearings tended to become more crowded and complex in their design. As we have seen, on family arms secondary charges were often added to the original one; or the shield was divided and subdivided into an increasingly large number of compartments, 'quarterings', combining a number of different arms within the confines of one shield. These divisions expressed relationships, ancestry and marriages or displayed the ownership of several fiefs, titles or rights. Some modern arms have ended up being illegible as a result of being quartered again and again; the grand quarters of Queen Victoria could have 256 quarterings.

Once they became marks of ownership and began to appear on countless objects of everyday life, arms

Geometrical designs can be divided into two groups: 'ordinaries' and 'lines of partition'. The lines of partition (above) are distinguished from the ordinaries (below) by the fact that they divide the shield into an even number of bands or compartments. The field of a shield divided by a line of partition forms a single plane. In the case of an ordinary, however, the charge is placed upon the field; there are two planes: the background field and the charge (such as a cross). Shields are divided and sub-divided into quarters and quarterings by the lines of partition; this makes it possible to combine several different arms on the same shield. The most common example is a division into four quarters (a 'quartered' shield). But the shield can also be divided into 16, 32, 64 or even 256 quarterings. The world record is the grand quarters of Lloyd of Stockton, divided up into 323 quarterings (right).

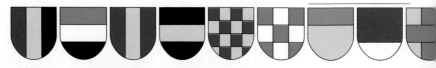

became smaller in comparison to those displayed on the banners and shields of the 12th-century combatants. Not only did they become difficult to decipher but their artistic effect also declined. In general the heraldic style, which reached its peak at the court of Burgundy in the 15th century, became less inventive, more mechanical and also more affected from the 17th century; it still showed some signs of vigour in the Baroque art of Austria, Bavaria and northern Italy. Elsewhere it was often cold and graceless, a victim of the theorists of heraldry who wanted to codify and

What is known as the *Armorial de la cour amoureuse* ('amorous court') (below, the arms of the Duke of Burgundy and the Duke of Bourbon), copied and painted in Paris around 1420, represents the highpoint of early 15th-century heraldic design. It is this firm and elegant style that some 20th-century artists have tried to rediscover, sometimes imbuing it with a more Germanic expressiveness, like the great German heraldist Otto Hupp (left, one of his designs).

lay down everything (composition, numbers, proportions) exactly, leaving no room for inventiveness and little for elegance. In the 20th century, however, several German (notably Otto Hupp), Swiss and Scandinavian artists have managed to restore to heraldic design the simplicity and force of expression it had in the Middle Ages.

Deciphering arms

Apart from quartering and the frequent combination of two arms on a single shield, another essential feature of armorial composition is its depth. Several levels are piled one on top of the other and they must be read starting from the lowest level. In fact, that is how most medieval images must be read, especially those from the late Romanesque period, when arms first appeared: first the lowest level, then the intermediary ones and finally the level nearest to the spectator's eye – an order that goes against the grain today. When designing armorial bearings, artists first choose a field, then charge it with a device; if they want to add other features they have to place them on the same level as the charge or – as frequently happens – superimpose a new level; it is impossible to go backwards. So the shield can be regarded as made up of a series of levels: the lowest represents the original structure and the main charges of the arms; the middle and top ones are charged with successive augmentations and help to distinguish between, for example, two branches of the same family or two individuals from the same branch.

All arms are constructed on a series of superimposed levels. Each charge added in the course of time had to be placed on the uppermost level, that is on the level nearest to the eye of the spectator, or form a new level. Here (diagonally, from page 66 to page 67) we see how the arms of Guillaume de Jeucourt, a Norman lord, took shape. First a field Or (lowest level); then a Cross Gules placed on this field (second level); then four Lions Sable in the quarterings of the cross (also on the second level); then a Roundel Argent placed on the cross (third level); finally, a Hammer Gules charging the Bezant (fourth level).

The crest: mask or totem?

The shield is the essential element of heraldic composition. In the strict sense of the word, it bears the arms. In the course of time, however, accessories were added to this shield, some purely decorative (helmets, coronets, mantling), others serving to indicate the identity, rank, office or dignity of the owner. But on the Continent these external elements were never governed by rules (though they were in England), unlike the tinctures and charges on the shield proper.

The earliest external ornament is the crest on the upper part of the helmet. Its origins go back as far as classical antiquity, where its function was military: to frighten the enemy, to make the combatant look bigger and to attract beneficial forces towards him. At the end of the Middle Ages it became mainly a ceremonial piece of decoration: worn at tournaments, rarely at war, it was a fragile structure of wood, boiled leather, canvas and plumes. When depicted on paintings or monuments, the crest above the shield was never represented realistically; sometimes it took on considerable proportions; sometimes it grew in number. For example, during the Baroque period, a shield divided into four quarters was even given four different crests.

When the earliest arms appeared, the knights used to paint their helmets in different tinctures, sometimes adding attributes (horns or wings) that were the first crests. It took several decades for these designs or motifs to become established with the same individual or family. For a long time people remained very free in their choice of crests. In the 15th century it was still quite common for a knight to change his crest for each tournament or for him to raise a totally imaginary crest in a joust. Left: a horned crest. Below: the canting crest of a lord from Baden (in German *Baden* means 'bath').

Over the centuries, in fact, the crest decoration on the helmet, which at first was individual and could be changed at will depending on circumstances or the whim of the user, tended to stay the same and become hereditary within one family. It could then repeat a charge displayed on the shield or, more frequently, consist of another charge.

In Germanic countries, family crests became established very early on and were often an essential part of the shield.

In Poland and Hungary the crest often acquired a 'totemic' function, with all the members of a family group using the same crest and the name of that crest being used as the surname of the entire dynasty.

Elsewhere, crests were used more flexibly and intended for display purposes, although many of them eventually became hereditary.

In England, for example, shields became so heavily charged and complex in the 18th and 19th centuries that the crest was often used more frequently than the arms.

Very few crested helmets have survived until our times. These fragile decorative elements usually disappeared in the course of combat. Left: a crested helmet from the early 15th century.

Church dignitaries rarely surmounted their shields with a crest. However, the crosses, mitres and caps distinguish clergymen from soldiers and, among the former, cardinals from bishops and bishops from ordinary canons.
Left: the arms of the ecclesiastical benefactors of the Abbey of Monte Cassino.

Collars, insignia and other devices

Other external ornaments include the 'supporters'. They first appeared on seals in the course of the 14th century and are made up of animal or human figures that appear to be holding up the shield. They have been used more widely in modern times but remain ornamental, even though some families have always tried to use the same supporters.

Conversely, the collars of orders of chivalry and the insignia of office and rank (episcopal cross, crosier, sword belonging to a *connétable*) are personal and significant. They help identify an individual when the armorial shield itself only indicates the family and they can often provide a certain amount of data on the life or career of that individual.

The many coronets that surmounted shields from the 17th century are, on the whole, decorative. There are five coronets of rank that may surmount the arms of English peers.

Finally, from the end of the Middle Ages, a motto, in the modern sense of the term, would sometimes be added to the shield. It could be a single word, derived from the war cries of feudal times, or an entire phrase. The mottoes were generally inscribed on a scroll or ribbon. Some are individual, some belong to a family or community. The same individual or family could have several mottoes, while the same motto could be common to several families, communities or unrelated individuals.

At the end of the Middle Ages in England, the leaders of military campaigns decorated their standards with a variety of emblems: livery colours, insignia of orders of knighthood, devices, badges, mottoes and pious invocations.

Left: two examples from the early 16th century belonging to Brian Stapleton and Henry Stafford. Stapleton's device is a wounded dog, accompanied by the enigmatic motto 'mievlx i ssera'; Stafford's is a collared, chained swan, a crescent on its breast, with the motto 'humble et loyal'. Mottoes of this kind disappeared during the 17th century, when collars of order and insignia of rank began to surround the shields of important personages (above, the arms of Cardinal Richelieu).

The term 'heraldry' derives from the word 'herald,' which itself stems from the Old High German *heriwald* and Old French *hérault*, meaning messenger. Its origin is not entirely certain. Heralds are first mentioned in about 1170. The term heraldry is often used as a synonym for armory, which is only one of the herald's duties.

CHAPTER 3

A MISUNDERSTOOD SCIENCE

Heraldry, seen everywhere, places its signs and codes on many different objects, whether on the shield and banner of Christ – crested with the instruments of the Passion – on a 15th-century manuscript (opposite) or on road signs (right); in fact they all respect its rules.

Scholarly heralds

Originally, the herald was an officer in the service of a prince or lord; his job was to carry messages, declare war and announce tournaments. Gradually he specialized in the latter task and, rather like a modern reporter, described to the spectator the main feats of arms of the participants in tournaments. In this way he deepened his knowledge of armorial bearings, for they and they alone made it possible to identify the jousters who were unrecognizable under their armour.

Gradually the heralds thus became real armorial experts; they codified the rules and the representation of arms; they determined the language to be used for describing them; they travelled throughout the West to record them and compile collections or rolls, in which they painted or drew the arms they had found.

In England there has been a long history of scholarly heralds, including Robert Glover in the 16th century, Sir William Dugdale and Elias Ashmore in the 17th century, John Anstis and Stephen Martin Leake in the 18th century, Sir George Nayler and William Courthope in the 19th century and Sir Anthony Wagner in the 20th century.

Arms provide a wealth of information of all kinds. In particular they reveal two aspects of their bearers: their identity and the social and cultural environment in which they lived. For a long time the main contribution of heraldry to political and dynastic history, genealogical studies, archaeology and history of art was in identifying the owners of arms.

From the 14th century, the heralds of arms wore a special garment, the tabard, a kind of tunic decorated with the arms of the lord they served. This garment is still worn today by the heralds in the service of the British Crown (below, an 18th-century tabard with the arms of George I, King of England and Scotland). Heralds of arms did not have the same influence on the development of heraldry in every place. It was strong in countries where arms had military origins (England, France, Netherlands, Rhineland and southern Germany), but was less so elsewhere (Italy, Spain, Portugal, Poland, Scandinavia).

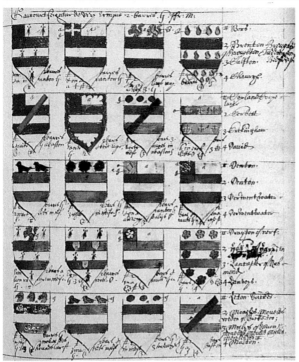

From the mid-16th century, scholars realized how useful heraldry was for the study of genealogical, dynastic and political history. They copied a large number of medieval arms and compiled new ones and began to list the coats of arms of particular families (left, those of an English family), towns or regions. These lists or rolls of arms were more numerous in the next century, when heraldry became a valuable aid to archaeology and philology. In France, where the wars of religion destroyed numerous monuments and works of art, some 'antiquaries', such as Nicolas Peiresc and Roger de Gaignières, undertook to have a large number of heraldic documents copied in order to preserve their memory and make them available to scholars.

A tool for genealogy and family history

As a social code heraldry, with its rules on the representation of arms, can often situate the individual within a group and that group within society as a whole. Those who can decipher arms can sometimes discover from them the position of an individual within a family, his or her matrimonial alliances, functions and social status, then the position of the family within a line of descent, its origins, the history of its alliances and descendants, the connections between different lineages, the history of their titles and possessions and that of the fiefs, dynasties, kingdoms or states.

Within the same family, only one individual, the eldest male of the eldest branch, bears the entire family arms. All the others, such as the sons of a living father or, if the father is deceased, the younger brothers of the eldest living son, have no right to do so and have to slightly modify the shield to show they are not head of the family, that is the eldest member of the eldest branch. This modification is called a mark of difference, mark of cadency or *brisure*. It does not apply to women: unmarried daughters bear the same arms as their father, while married women generally bear arms that combine the arms of their husband and their father within the same shield.

Marks of difference are mainly found in the 'classic'

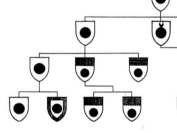

heraldic countries, that is those where arms appeared on the battlefields in the 12th century: England, Scotland, France, the Netherlands, Rhineland Germany and Switzerland. Elsewhere they are more rare (Scandinavia, Austria, Spain) or very rare (Italy, Poland). Marks of difference on family arms can take various forms: the addition or subtraction of a charge, a change of tincture or the inversion of the tincture of the field and that of the charge. Initially, these differences were well accepted socially and therefore conspicuous. Later, the younger

When the system of differences is strictly observed within a family, the coats of arms of the younger branches become, over the generations, increasingly different from those of the eldest branch.

REINES DE FRANCE DEPUIS FARAMOND IUSQU'A PRESENT

The French royal family, like the English one, always paid due respect to the use of marks of difference, even in the 18th century, a time when they had fallen into disuse in many noble families. However, over the centuries the marks of difference of the French royal family became increasingly discreet (left, armorial genealogy of the King of France drawn up by Jacques Chevillard), while they remained very marked in England and Scotland. Opposite: genealogical diagram of the Stodart family.

Marks of difference based on changes or inversions of tincture were not uncommon

members of a family became less keen to proclaim this fact loudly and preferred a more discreet difference, usually in the form of the addition of a small charge.

Since arms are inherited, it can happen that after several generations and a succession of marks of difference the arms of the younger branches no longer resemble the arms of the eldest branch. Sometimes, however, the resemblance between the arms of two apparently unrelated families reveals that they have a common ancestor. Heraldry is therefore a valuable tool for genealogy. It helps to establish pedigrees, to rebuild relationships, to distinguish between those who share the same name.

in the Middle Ages. Above: an example from the Norman Malet family, taken from a 15th-century armorial. Later they became exceptional, no doubt because they looked too garish.

A useful tool for art history and archaeology

As both marks of ownership and decorative ornaments, arms were displayed from the 12th to the 19th centuries on countless objects, monuments and documents, to which they thereby gave a kind of civil status. The study of heraldry is indeed at times the only means available today to situate these objects and monuments in space and time, to discover who commissioned them and their successive owners, to trace their history and the course of events. Once identified – a difficult exercise, but one of the main tasks of the heraldist – arms become documents that are much prized by archaeologists and art historians.

The most valuable contribution of heraldry is in dating, for the period during which an individual bore an armorial shield was usually shorter than his life span. And when it is a question of a king or a prince in whose arms each quartering represents the ownership of a fief or principality, it is possible to be even more precise by seeking the reasons and events underlying the structure of the arms in question. At times, heraldry can date an object to within a few months, especially where objects, works of art or monuments are decorated with several shields belonging to several different individuals: a date can be established on the basis of the dates of birth, marriage, start of 'reign', tenure of title or office and death of each armiger. One famous example is the small 13th-century enamelled coffer housed in the

The casket of St Louis was discovered in the church of Dammarie-les-Lys in 1853. It is a tin-plated, wooden coffer decorated with crystal cabochons and gilt and enamelled medallions depicting people, animals and arms. For a long time scholars dated this object to the late 13th century and considered it to be one of the coffers in which Philip the Fair of France placed certain relics of St Louis after his canonization in 1297. But this dating does not agree with that of the arms. A contemporary heraldist, Hervé Pinoteau, therefore reviewed the entire question and suggested an earlier date: 1236. He began by identifying each of the forty-six surviving armorial shields; he then determined a date on the basis of the dates of death, marriage, dubbing and beginning of reign, office, title or function of each of the individuals depicted. They were all relatives or friends of St Louis.

The narrowest time span this gave dates these arms to the summer of 1236. This is a fine example of the way heraldry can help to date and attribute objects.

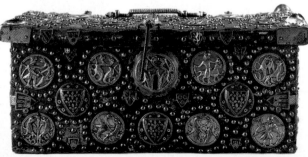

Louvre and known as the casket of St Louis: art history could not date it to within less than fifty years, but, thanks to the research undertaken by Hervé Pinoteau, heraldry managed to pinpoint its manufacture to within a period of a few weeks.

What arms can tell us

This archaeological aspect of heraldic studies forms part of what is called traditional heraldry. It looks mainly at the identity of the persons using the arms. But arms not only reveal the identity of their bearers: they can also reflect their personality. Heraldry is now branching out and devoting itself to that field of study.

Following the breakdown of the barriers between the various social sciences, over the past twenty years or so the science of heraldry has reformed the methods and widened the scope of armorial studies. For instance, it studies the

Armorial bearings help to identify each person shown on the Paumgartner altarpiece painted by Dürer in the early 16th century. Left: a 15th-century gold coin with the Visconti arms.

reasons governing the choice of tinctures and charges in order to discover the aspirations, beliefs, culture or sentiments of those who bore them or designed them.

Some of these reasons are impossible to establish and it must be admitted that about half of all European arms borne between the Middle Ages and the 18th century cannot be interpreted. But others reflect intentions that are more or less easy to identify, as when vassals adopted the same arms as their lord, or changed the tinctures, or when towns represented one of their monuments or one of the attributes of their patron saint on their arms. Or again, in the arms of corporations, the heraldic charge may directly evoke the craft or trade in question: the cow of the butcher, the squirrel of the furrier, the scissors of the tailor.

From names to images: canting arms

This applies in particular to what are known as canting arms or allusive arms, that is arms of which some components represent a pun or play on words on the name of the individual, family or community using them. This component is generally a charge, but can also be a tincture; for instance the Florentine Rossi family has an entirely red shield. The link can be direct – a family called Lecoq that bears a shield charged with a cock; phonetic – the city of Lille (formerly spelled and pronounced Lisle) has borne a fleur-de-lis since the 12th century; based on a rebus or pictorial pun – the Swiss Henneberg family bears a hen (in German *Henne*) perched on a mountain

The fleur-de-lis of the city of Florence is an allusive charge that appeared in the 13th century. Unlike that of the King of France, it is almost always shown in full bloom, with clearly marked stamens. Above: a 14th-century florin.

The presence of armorial bearings on medieval and modern coins means that heraldry is a very valuable tool for numismatics. It is also useful for studying the history of books. The study of bookplates, in particular, can help identify bibliophiles and reconstruct their libraries. Left: two contemporary bookplates, the upper one designed by the Swedish heraldist Jan Raneke, the lower one by the Swiss artist Paul Boesch.

(*Berg*); or more or less allusive – in Geneva the arms of the Le Fort (Strong One) family are charged with an elephant. The allusion can be crystal clear or derive from rare, obsolete or dialect words. That is why many canting arms are not recognized as such.

A large window depicting the arms of members of a corporation of boatmen from Switzerland.

But they are very common, accounting for perhaps twenty or twenty-five per cent of European arms in general, and even more in the Germanic countries. Contrary to what is sometimes alleged, canting arms were neither later than others nor confined largely to commoners. They were numerous from the outset and very frequent among the arms of the nobility. Even kingdoms used canting arms: the castle of the kingdom of Castile, for instance, or the lion of the kingdom of León. The study of canting arms is always highly informative. In the field of the study of names, for example, it enables the researcher to analyse the formation and development of certain family names and their relationship with the emblems concerned. It has emerged that the name did not always precede the arms but that, on the contrary, sometimes the habit of using a particular heraldic charge eventually led to the adoption of a family name. There are a number of examples of this in Scandinavia and around the Baltic. Similarly, in relation to the study of symbols, it is interesting to examine why some animals tended to be chosen as canting figures (such as the cock or the raven), while others were entirely disregarded, even when their name lent itself to it (such as the cat or the fox). The large German family of the Katzenellenbogen, for example, whose name evokes the cat (*Katze*), carefully avoided this animal, which was associated with the devil, as its heraldic emblem.

The arms of the Katzenellenbogen family.

Many allusive arms were created in German-speaking countries based on the name of a family. Sometimes they consist of a real rebus or pictorial pun, like those of the Swiss family of Helfenstein. Left: from a 14th-century armorial roll, charged with an elephant (*Elefant*) perched on a stone (*Stein*).

The new heraldry: fashion and taste

The new heraldry goes beyond the study of individual cases and also uses quantitative and statistical methods – in western Europe, medieval documents provide evidence of about one million different arms, while modern ones list more than ten million – in order to indicate the frequency or rarity of the incidence of charges and tinctures on the arms of a certain period, region, social class or group. By interpreting the findings obtained and comparing them with those produced by other disciplines, heraldry highlights the importance of fashion and taste and becomes an aspect of the history of cultural systems and perceptions.

An examination of the incidence of the various tinctures, for example, reveals a surprising emphasis on the colour blue throughout the West between the 13th and the 18th centuries; in arms, as in clothing and every social code, over the centuries blue was chosen in preference to red, the primordial colour. Indeed, even today it is by far the preferred colour of Europeans, whereas the Romans considered it 'barbaric' and at the time of Charlemagne no king or count wore blue. Heraldry provides firm evidence of this trend, which began in feudal times; it even enables this fashion to be studied on a numerical basis, century by century, decade by decade.

William Shakespeare, whose knowledge of arms is clear from his plays, bore the arms granted to his father in 1596. They were of course allusive arms: 'Or on a Bend Sable a Spear Or the point steeled proper'. Below: a late, inaccurate copy of Shakespeare's arms.

The Armorial Bearings of
WILLIAM SHAKESPEARE
of Stratford-upon-Avon.

The diagram below shows the comparative incidence of the main tinctures used in European arms.

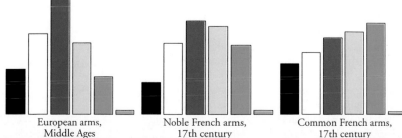

| European arms, Middle Ages | Noble French arms, 17th century | Common French arms, 17th century |

Good and evil heraldic charges

Similarly, the analysis of the incidence of particular heraldic charges provides information on cultural trends that goes far beyond the boundaries of heraldry.

The first example is the political opposition between the eagle and the lion in the arms of the Holy Roman Empire in the 12th and 13th centuries: the eagle was often the heraldic emblem of the supporters of the emperor and the lion that of his adversaries.

Then there is the bear, which was considered the king of the beasts in much of northern Europe until the end of the 13th century; even then, when the lion had supplanted the bear as king of the beasts everywhere else in folklore and zoological tradition, some German and Danish families whose name derived from the word *König* (Königsbach, Königsberger, etc.) continued to adopt canting arms charged with a bear rather than a lion.

Then there is the markedly pejorative nature of some of the animals (such as the monkey, the dragon, the snake, the frog – all animals of the devil) depicted on literary or imaginary arms that were attributed to individuals regarded as evil or of some shields charged with striped or chequered devices: to the medieval

Penthesilea, Queen of the Amazons, in full heraldic dress on the small equestrian armorial bearings of the Golden Fleece (c. 1440).

mind they were ambiguous or evil forms.

Finally, in both England and France a snobbish attitude developed in the 17th and 18th centuries, with commoners choosing particular charges (the rose, unicorn, fleur-de-lis), or, even more often, transforming charges regarded as common into charges that looked more important: dogs were turned into lions, cocks into eagles, pigs into boars, tools into weapons or even fleurs-de-lis.

Signs and dreams: imaginary heraldry

Today, however, the richest field of enquiry opened up by the new heraldry is certainly that of imaginary arms. That is the term used for arms attributed by the medieval and modern mind to individuals who never existed or who lived before the emergence of arms: literary or mythological heroes, biblical and Greco-Roman figures (David, Alexander, Caesar…), emperors, kings

The Middle Ages invented armorial bearings for the devil: Three Frogs Vert. These were regarded as signs of evil, as were indented lines at times (below).

and pops of the late
Middle Ages (especially
Charlemagne), personifi-
cations of the vices and
virtues. The range is very
wide and even saints and
divinities were endowed with
arms. The arms of Christ are
attested early on by several
documents: they take the
form of a shield charged
sometimes with a Paschal
lamb, sometimes with one
or more instruments of the
Passion. At the end of the
Middle Ages God himself was
attributed arms: a Bavarian
manuscript describes how
they were charged with a
symbolic image of the Trinity – in the form of a Y –
with a dove as crest. In fact, heraldry occupied such
an important position in the material and cultural life

The arms of God:
the symbol of the
Trinity surmounted by
a crest with a dove.

of the Germanic countries in the 15th and 16th centuries that absolutely anything could be endowed with arms.

The study of imaginary arms is proving a very rich source of information on heraldic symbolism. Relating what the people of a particular period knew or imagined about an individual with the charges and tinctures they attributed to him is of great help to the historian in the study of their symbolic value. As we have seen, this is more difficult with genuine arms, where fashion and taste play a greater part than the actual symbolic devices do.

Literary arms: from Chrétien de Troyes to Sir Walter Scott

The main imaginary arms are to be found in literary texts. At the end of the 12th century, for instance, Chrétien de Troyes and his successors blazoned the arms of King Arthur and the Knights of the Round Table. During the Renaissance, novelists, poets (Ariosto, Tasso) and playwrights (Shakespeare) still did the same, sometimes with a touch of irony – Rabelais, for instance, scoffed openly at heraldry in his *Gargantua* and Cervantes endowed Don Quixote with ridiculous arms. Even in the 19th century, major writers, such as Sir Walter Scott in England or Honoré de Balzac in France, attributed imaginary arms to many of their protagonists. For these writers, as for Chrétien de Troyes nearly seven centuries earlier, this was a means of emphasizing certain personality traits of an individual or announcing an

The attribution of arms to imaginary beings occurred in several stages. Starting in the 12th century, literary figures were given armorial shields and banners, which were blazoned in the text; later, the arms were also illustrated (opposite top left, the arms of Aeneas, hero of the *Aeneid*). Then legendary saints, biblical and mythological figures and divinities were endowed with arms. Finally, in the late Middle Ages, the personifications of the vices and virtues were also attributed arms (above, a tapestry depicting the arms of Chastity: a shield charged with an angel, a crest with a dove, a banner with a unicorn).

In the Middle Ages, the largest and most coherent body of literary arms were those of the Knights of the Round Table. Lancelot, Gawain, Percival, Galahad, Tristan and a few others were attributed arms at the end of the 12th century or the beginning of the 13th century. Within a few decades, many of their companions had also received them. By the 15th century some 150 to 180 Knights of the Round Table bore arms, now listed in special armorials. In illuminated manuscripts, each

episode to come in the story, or simply as a hint to the reader.

Among these literary and imaginary arms, the most stable – those of King Arthur and his knights, of Alexander, Caesar, Charlemagne and a few others – soon spread from texts to works of art and images. As iconographical attributes, they help identify the bearer.

De ſynople briſé a vn filet, & 3. lambeaux d'argent en chef. Par quelques vns, de ſynople à vn lambeau à trois pendans d'argent.

hero can thus be identified by his shield. Top left: Mador de la Porte (left) and Lancelot (right).

The language of blazon: rigorous and poetic

Finally, the new heraldry proposes to study the language of blazon in both linguistic and semiotic terms, as a documentary language and a system of signs. This language, which has its own vocabulary and grammar, is highly efficient: although made up of only a few elements, it provides much information. Depending on the country, it is more or less intelligible to the layman. It is in France and the United Kingdom that we find the widest disparity between everyday language and the language of heraldry: the layman can understand very little of a description of arms in the language of blazon. This is particularly true of English heraldry, which still uses Anglo-Norman as it was spoken and written in the 12th and 13th centuries. In Italy and Spain the gap is slightly narrower. In Germany, the Netherlands and Scandinavia it is even smaller and the terms used for the tinctures and the grammatical conventions are closer to those of everyday language.

In the United Kingdom and France, this 'dislocation' was in fact a gradual process. In the 13th century, the heralds of arms who described the arms of the participants in a tournament to the spectators were still understood by educated people. The heraldic language was the same as that used in literary texts. But in the 15th century,

D'or, brifé en chef d'vne mollette d'efperon de fable.

when the first blazon treatises were written, the heralds deliberately made the language so complicated that they themselves were indispensable.

The 17th-century scholars added further complications and unnecessary details. Finally, in the 19th century, many heraldists fell into the trap of pedantry and finally made any description of arms unintelligible to the layman.

Today the language of blazon deserves to attract greater curiosity on the part of linguists. Not only does it say much with little, not only does it look like an extremely elaborate code, but it is the language

King Arthur was the main hero created by the medieval mind. But for the men and women of the Middle Ages he was a very real person who formed part of their everyday life: many texts, plays, entertainments, pictures and documents tell the story of King Arthur, Queen Guinevere and the Knights of the Round Table. Arthur was attributed arms at an early date: Azure three Crowns Or (above, on a 14th-century tapestry).

Arms are still very much alive in the towns and cities of England and Scotland – not just those that past centuries have handed down to us on many monuments, but also more recently created ones that serve as the emblems of municipal or government institutions, banks, insurance companies, businesses, colleges, sports clubs or even pubs or brands of beer.

best suited to describing heraldic images, always giving priority to structure over form. It also has a great poetic and suggestive power: 'Sable three hunting Horns Or', 'Ermine a Fess dancetty Vert', 'Azure a Lion rampant Argent armed and langued Or the tail forked and in Saltire', 'Checky Or and Gules on a Pale between two Pales Vair a Cross recercely Purpure'.

Modern heraldry: from arms to logos

After a period of decline between the two world wars, there has been a marked revival of interest in heraldic studies in most of western Europe over the past thirty years or so. University researchers and archivists are now showing more interest in arms than their predecessors. Moreover, thanks to the increasing use of computers, they can greatly widen the scope of their research and investigations.

But heraldry is not just the prerogative of scholars. It is also a part of everyday life. In some countries (Switzerland or Scotland, for example) there has in fact never been any break between medieval and contemporary heraldry: arms have continued to be displayed on many monuments and, over the centuries, taken up

Among the various contemporary systems of signs, the international code of signals has the closest links with heraldry. It uses a different flag for each number and for each letter of the alphabet. These flags, designed to be seen from afar, are constructed like genuine arms: five basic tinctures (green is not used) that strictly observe the rules of blazon, and entirely heraldic ordinaries and lines of partition. This code was born at sea and is still used mainly for signalling by ships. Its main application is to signal the various manoeuvres a ship is about to carry out or to tell what is happening on board. Some 'alphabetical' flags also send out specific messages: for instance the flag corresponding to the letter 'O' also means 'man overboard'.

more and more space. In others, it is mainly the arms of corporate bodies, especially cities, that continue to reflect the presence of heraldry in everyday life. Today this urban heraldry is very much alive and has sometimes, as in Scandinavia, given rise to highly original works.

However, the influence of heraldry is not just found on arms. It is also reflected in flags, direct descendants of the heraldry system – nearly all the flags of the world respect the heraldic rules on tincture combinations: in logos, which in some cases compete crudely with arms and are often based on canting charges, and even in road signs, designed as genuine arms that scrupulously respect heraldic rules regarding the use of tincture, both in Europe and worldwide.

The 'Argent a Square Billet Azure' flag (above, second flag from top) corresponds to the letter 'P' and means the ship is about to sail.

Legacies of heraldry

Heraldry has had an even stronger influence on sports:

Many cars are fitted with small badges. Some are genuine arms, such as the arms of the Dukes of Milan on Alfa Romeo cars or those of the Dukes of

badges, flags and banners, sports shirts, the scarves and streamers waved by the fans, all these are heraldic, sometimes prolonging the life of century-old insignia and emblems without the players or spectators really being aware of it. For example, few people know that the colours of the two prestigious Milan football clubs (Inter and AC Milan) were the emblematic tinctures of two districts of that city in the 16th century.

Sometimes the roots of our emblems, insignia and logos lie even deeper. At the end of the 13th century, Otto IV, Count of Burgundy, gave up his family arms, charged with an eagle, and adopted a shield charged with a lion. In so doing, he wanted to announce that he had broken all ties with the emperor, his sovereign. This lion shield was retained by all his successors and became, in modern times, the shield of Franche-Comté,

which covers the same territory as the original county of Burgundy. At the end of the 19th century, the heraldic lion of Franche-Comté found its way on to the cars built by the Peugeot company, which adopted it as its emblem because its headquarters and factories were in the Montbéliard region of that country. So if the Count of Burgundy had not quarrelled with the Emperor of Germany six centuries

Württemberg on Porsche cars. Others repeat the heraldic charges of famous arms, such as the lion borrowed from the arms of Franche-Comté on the Peugeot car.

earlier, the emblem of one of the most prosperous French car manufacturers might have been quite different today. It could have been an eagle, at the risk of shocking the French buyers of the beginning of the century who would immediately have equated it with the Prussian emblem. We can be sure that in the context of the period the lion of the counts of Burgundy had some influence on the fortunes of Armand Peugeot.

Heraldry is also seen on the sports field, in the colours used by the different teams and the badges on their shirts. Below: the rugby player Nick Farr-Jones, wearing the Australian national shirt.

Overleaf: still from *Henry V* (1988).

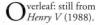

DOCUMENTS

Do historians fear the fleur-de-lis?

The scarcity of specialist works devoted to the fleur-de-lis may well justify this question. Yet the fleur-de-lis is an authentic historical object that is at one and the same time political, dynastic, artistic, emblematic and symbolic. It is far from neutral and the various ideologies surrounding its study in France since the birth of the republic have created mistrust among historians and archaeologists.

Even heraldists have shown some reluctance and have not yet produced the kind of consolidated work on this symbol of the French monarchy that would rightly be expected of them.

Yet there are enough documents: from the 12th to the 19th centuries the fleur-de-lis appears everywhere, giving rise to a great many problems…. It is time medievalists resumed their investigations and looked into the scientific questions involved in order to provide studies of the history of this flower that are as solid and fruitful as those on the history of the German eagle, the English, Belgian and Dutch lions and the Scandinavian crosses.

Most authors who have written on the graphic origins of the fleur-de-lis agree that it bears little relation to the real lily, but differ as to whether it is derived from the iris, the lotus, the flowers of broom or gorse or – an even more extravagant hypothesis – whether it represents a trident, the point of an arrow, an axe or even a dove. In my view this is a question of little importance. The point is that it is a stylized device, certainly a flower, which has been used as an ornamental motif or an emblematic attribute by many societies in the Old and the New World. In fact, it is found on Mesopotamian cylinder seals, Egyptian bas-reliefs and Mycenaean pottery, as it is on Gallic coins, Sassanid fabrics, Amero-Indian clothing and Japanese arms. However, the symbolic meaning of this flower varies from culture to culture. Sometimes it is a symbol of purity or virginity, sometimes a sign of fertility and fecundity, sometimes an insignia of power or sovereignty.

The earliest examples of fleurs-de-lis similar to those used in Europe in the

Seal of Lille.

Gradually a Marian symbolism was grafted on to this Christological dimension, linked to the development of the worship of the Virgin, to which the following line from the Song of Solomon was henceforth taken to refer: 'As the lily among thorns, so is my love among the daughters' (Song of Sol. 2:2), and to numerous passages from the Scriptures and patristic texts in which the lily is presented as a symbol of purity and virginity.

With time the lily thus became an attribute of the Virgin. The first representations are found on coins: several 11th- and 12th-century coins issued by bishops whose cathedral church was dedicated to the Virgin depict fleurs-de-lis in the field. Then the chapters of these same churches displayed images of the Virgin carrying a lily in her right hand on their seals: Notre Dame of Paris from 1146, Notre Dame of Noyon in 1174, Notre Dame of Laon in 1181. The chapters were soon followed by the abbeys and priories. Henceforth, there are countless iconographical representations of the Virgin holding, or surrounded by, lilies. Sometimes they are simple fleurons, sometimes garden lilies, sometimes genuine heraldic fleurs-de-lis, sometimes depicted on a sceptre, crown or mantle flory or floretty. This fashion seems to have reached its peak in the 13th century. In the late Middle Ages, however, the lily began to be rivalled by the rose as the floral attribute of the Virgin in Marian iconography. The flower of love seemed to be taking precedence over the flower of virginity.

The Capetian fleur-de-lis

Much study has been devoted to the date, reasons and significance of the choice by the kings of France of the

Arms with fleurs-de-lis.

Middle Ages and in modern times are found on Assyrian bas-reliefs of the 3rd millennium BC. They decorate tiaras, necklaces and sceptres and already seem to serve as royal attributes. Those found a little later in Crete, India and Egypt probably had a similar significance. The fleur-de-lis is then found on a number of Greek, Roman and Gallic coins. However, whereas in the first two cases the design is fairly unstable, in the latter it is almost a genuine heraldic fleur-de-lis.

An attribute of the Virgin Mary

While remaining a royal attribute, in the early Middle Ages the fleur-de-lis also acquired a strong Christological dimension. Its origin can be found in the line from the Song of Solomon, so often studied and commented on by the Church Fathers and theologians: 'I am the rose of Sharon, and the lily of the valleys' (Song of Sol. 2:1). For this reason, the figure of Christ was, until the 13th century, often shown surrounded by lilies or stylized fleurons.

fleur-de-lis as their heraldic emblem. Several writers commented on it from the second half of the 13th century, while throughout the next century a number of literary works – mainly intended to legitimize the right of the Valois to the throne – explained that the King of France 'bears arms of three

T he arms of the dauphin.

fleur-de-lis as a sign of the Trinity; the angel of God sent them to Clovis, the first Christian king…telling him to scrape off the arms with three frogs that he bore on his shield and replace them with three fleurs-de-lis'.

This legend remained widespread until the late 16th century. Henceforth fleurs-de-lis were no longer regarded as the expression of the three virtues, faith, wisdom and chivalry (the interpretation given to the three petals of the flower at the time of St Louis), but as the actual symbol of the Trinity, guardian of the kingdom of France. They were sent from heaven to Clovis, the founding king of the monarchy, when he converted to Christianity and

immediately replaced the frogs – eminently diabolical charges – on the arms he supposedly bore before his baptism.

This tradition proved very hardy. Despite the attacks by 17th-century scholars it was still repeated by 19th-century historians. Today, of course, the opinion of *ancien régime* scholars is no longer disputed: there were no arms, anywhere in Europe, before the first half of the 12th century and the King of France was certainly not one of the first princes to bear them. In fact, it is not until the year 1211 that we find a seal depicting a Capetian prince bearing the famous shield strewn with fleurs-de-lis. And that was not even King Philippe Auguste (1180–1223) himself but his oldest son, Prince Louis, the future Louis VIII (1223–6)….

Under the influence of Abbot Suger, advisor to Louis VI (1108–37), then Louis VII (1137–80) and St Bernard (1091–1153), who both had a strong devotion to the Virgin and wanted to place the kingdom of France under her protection, Louis VI, followed by Louis VII, gradually introduced the fleurs-de-lis into their repertoire of symbols and then gave them a special place among the emblems of the French monarchy. In the second half of the reign of Louis VII, the most pious of the first Capetian kings, this flower was increasingly put to ideological ends. By then the king of France was using it more frequently than any other Christian sovereign. Finally, a few decades later, at the beginning of Philippe Auguste's reign, when an emblem was sought for the royal arms that were evolving, it was only natural to think of the charge that had been closely linked to the Capetian monarchy and the Virgin for two reigns. Henceforth, like the mother of Christ, with whom he shared this floral attribute, the Capetian king really could claim to be the mediator between heaven and earth, between God and the subjects of his kingdom….

A shared flower

The King of France, his family and officials were not the only ones to use fleurs-de-lis on their arms. Far from it. By the end of the 12th century this flower had become a fully fledged heraldic charge common to most of western Europe. Only the lion, the eagle and two or three geometrical charges are more frequently found on arms.

The fleur-de-lis did, however, show a preference for certain geographical areas: the northern and southern Netherlands, Brittany, Poitou, Bavaria and Tuscany. In terms of social class, it is found mainly on the arms of the aristocracy and the gentry and on the para-heraldic arms and emblems of peasants. It is the most common charge on peasants' seals.

In France under the *ancien régime*, there were many attempts to explain the presence of fleurs-de-lis on the arms of particular families, individuals or communities. Several writers, often paid by those who actually possessed the arms, did not hesitate to create legends and glorious ancestries, suggesting a distant relationship with the Capetian dynasty or imagining a great service to the Crown, for which the king had granted them arms. In truth, none of this is based on historical fact. It was very rare for the kings of France to grant fleurs-de-lis. There is one early example: in 1389 King Charles VI authorized his 'cousin' Charles of Albret, the future *connétable* of France, to quarter the arms of France and those of Albret on the same shield.

Yet, in the vast majority of cases, the presence of fleurs-de-lis on a shield is due simply to its frequent incidence as a heraldic charge.

Often it has the same technical function on arms as other small charges such as stars, bezants (circular charges), annulets, crescents, martlets (small stylized birds without feet or claws): it accompanies, or is charged upon, geometrical charges and it fills a monochrome field. As always in heraldry, fashions are more geographical than social.

On certain arms, however, the fleur-de-lis can be a 'canting' charge, that is it can constitute a play on words on the name of the private individual or corporate body using the arms. The allusion can be based on the word flower ('flos' in Latin), as in the case of the arms of Florence, or on the word lily ('lilium' in Latin), as in the arms of Lille, known from a late 12th-century seal and still present on the emblem of that city.

Michel Pastoureau
'Le roi aux fleurs de lis'
in *L'Histoire*, January 1995

The eagle and the lion in medieval arms

Arms are emblems that contain a great many codes. They therefore lend themselves well to statistical analysis and the findings can be set out in tables or maps. Maps show how the incidence of certain charges and tinctures varies according to country and region rather than social class or group.

Maps showing the incidence of the various heraldic charges often prove highly revealing. The two maps opposite, relating to the eagle and the lion, are based on a statistical survey of some 25,000 medieval arms (12th–15th centuries) throughout Europe.

The boundaries demarcate the main fiefs or groups of fiefs at the end of the 14th century. Despite the differences of incidence (the lion is by far the most common charge on arms), it becomes quite apparent that, apart from Spain, in regions where the lion is common the eagle is uncommon and vice versa. In medieval heraldry the two animals were regarded as opposites, although both were insignia of power. In much of 13th-century Europe there seems to have been a division of loyalty between the eagle (supporters of the emperor) and the lion (his adversaries), so that many noblemen adopted the eagle or the lion as their charge for political reasons.

The eagle/lion opposition is in fact reminiscent of the emblematic opposition between the bear and the boar in the Celtic and Germanic civilizations of the High Middle Ages.

Michel Pastoureau
'L'héraldique nouvelle'
Pour la science, November 1977

Eagle arms: more than 15%, 12–15%, 10–12%, 5–10%, less than 5%.

Lion arms: more than 70%, 60–70%, 50–60%, 30–50%, less than 35% (the higher the percentage, the darker the shading).

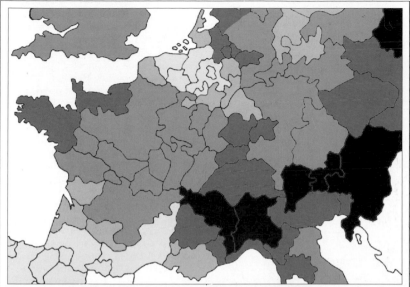

Percentage of eagle arms (above) and lion arms (below) in relation to the total number of animal arms in the same region.

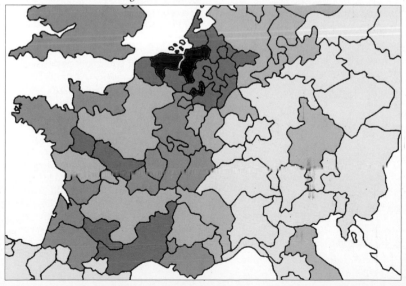

A 14th-century case about the right to bear arms

In the 12th and 13th centuries, when the composition of arms was still very simple (one charge, two tinctures), it was quite common for two families who were not related to bear similar arms. From the 14th century on, however, such cases were tolerated less and less. Some families would ask their prince or king to arbitrate and decide who was to retain the arms in question and who had to change them.

One of the most interesting and important incidents in the history of heraldry in England was the three-party dispute between Scrope, Grosvenor and Carminow. This case is little known outside England.

In 1385, when Richard II invaded Scotland, two of his knights, Sir Richard Scrope of Bolton in Yorkshire and Sir Robert Grosvenor of Cheshire, found they bore the same shield, 'dazure ove une bende dore' [Azure a Bend Or]. Scrope brought an action but Grosvenor maintained that Sir Gilbert Grosvenor had come to England with William the Conqueror bearing arms of a Bend Or and that since then all his ancestors had always borne them. The case was heard before the *curia militaris*, presided over by the *connétable* of England. Several hundred witnesses were heard and among those who gave evidence for Scrope were Jean de Gand, King of Castile and Duke of Lancaster, his son Henry (the future Henry IV) and the poet Geoffrey Chaucer. The case dragged on. Finally, in 1389 the *connétable* found in Scrope's favour, while granting Grosvenor permission to bear 'les ditz armes ove un playn bordure d'argent' [the said arms within a plain Bordure Argent]. This finding displeased both Scrope and Grosvenor and the latter appealed to the King. Richard II gave his personal verdict on 27 May 1390, confirming Scrope's right to bear the Bend Or and annulling the permission the *connétable* had given Grosvenor to bear the bend differenced by a Bordure Argent. One of the reasons the King gave for this annulment was that this Bordure was 'not a sufficient difference in arms between two strangers in blood in one kingdom'; it was only sufficient as a difference 'between cousin and cousin in blood'.

The presentation of arms to heralds (opposite) and detail (above).

Several witnesses referred to a third person, Thomas Carminow of Cornwall, who bore arms 'Azure a Bend Or' in 1360, during the expedition to France. At that time Carminow's right to bear these arms had already been disputed by Grosvenor. Nobody knows how this case ended but clearly the two adversaries continued to use the Bend without any modification. On another occasion, during the same case, Carminow challenged Scrope's right to bear the Bend Or. This time, the case was judged immediately by the *connétable* assisted by six knights, who decided that both Scrope and Carminow had established their right. It is quite amusing to note that, according to the judges, Carminow had proved that his ancestors had borne the arms with a Bend Or since the time of King Arthur, Scrope only since the Norman Conquest (1066).

Since the 1390 judgment, the Scrope and Carminow families have borne the Bend Or without interruption. Grosvenor, however, had to choose a new shield, and he adopted Azure a Garb Or, arms still borne today by his descendant, the Duke of Westminster.

Some modern writers have said that Carminow and Grosvenor fought physically over their controversy. In fact, the three disputes were decided by law. The error no doubt stems from a misinterpretation of the term 'challenge'. In modern English 'challenge' sometimes means to challenge to a duel, but its usual meaning is to dispute or call into question and it is in that sense that we must interpret 'challenge'.

H. S. London
'La controverse Scrope-Grosvenor-Carminow'
in *Archives héraldiques suisses*, 1951

Heraldry in Britain

Examples of heraldry can be found in many areas of British life, including its literature and its flag.

Many poets and novelists have described arms, although they were not always familiar with the rules of blazon. Malory's Le Morte d'Arthur, *the classic treatment of chivalry, was written c. 1470 and was among the first books printed by Caxton in 1485. The heraldry in it is relatively simple.*

And within a while after there came a squire of the castle, that told Sir Pellounes, that was lord of that castle, that a knight with a black shield had smitten down thirteen knights.

'Fair brother,' said Sir Tristram unto Sir Persides, 'let us cast upon us cloaks, and let us go see the play.'

'Not so,' said Sir Persides, 'we will not go like knaves thither, but we will ride like men and good knights to withstand our enemies.'

So they armed them, and took their horses and great spears, and thither they went thereas many knights assayed themself before the tournament.

And anon Sir Palomides saw Sir Persides, and then he sent a squire unto him and said: 'Go thou to the yonder knight with the green shield and therein a lion of gules, and say him I require him to joust with me, and tell him that my name is Sir Palomides.'

When Sir Persides understood that request of Sir Palomides, he made him ready, and there anon they met together, but Sir Persides had a fall.

Then Sir Tristram dressed him to be revenged upon Sir Palomides, and that saw Sir Palomides that was ready and so was not Sir Tristram, and took him at an advantage and smote him over his horse's tail when he had no spear in his rest.

Thomas Malory
Le Morte d'Arthur, Book IX, Ch. 27
c. 1470

Shakespeare was familiar with arms and there are many allusions to them in his plays.

Petruchio: Good Kate; I am a gentleman.
Katherina: That I'll try. [She strikes him.]
Petruchio: I swear I'll cuff you, if you strike again.
Katherina: So may you lose your arms.
If you strike me, you are no gentleman;
And if no gentleman, why then no arms.
Petruchio: A herald, Kate? O, put me in thy books!
Katherina: What is your crest – a coxcomb?
Petruchio: A combless cock, so Kate will be my hen.

William Shakespeare
The Taming of the Shrew
Act II, scene 1, 1593

The tournament in Nashe's The Unfortunate Traveller, *in which the Earl of Surrey challenges all-comers to maintain the superior beauty of his mistress, is a parody of courtly romances and tales of chivalry. Nine contenders are described in great detail. Nashe's humour at the expense of unintelligible mottoes and obscure symbolism tends itself to be rather unintelligible and obscure to the modern reader, but the fertility of his invention is impressive.*

The sixth was the Knight of the Storms, whose helmet was round-moulded like the moon, and all his armour like waves, whereon the shine of the moon, slightly silvered, perfectly represented moon-shine in the water. His bases were the banks or shores that bounded in the streams. The spoke was this, *Frustra pius*, as much to say as 'fruitless service'. On his shield he set forth a lion driven from his prey by a dunghill cock. The word, *Non vi sed voce*: 'not by violence but by voice'.

The seventh had, like the giants that sought to scale heaven in despite of Jupiter, a mount overwhelming his head and whole body; his bases outlaid with arms and legs which the skirts of that mountain left uncovered. Under this did he characterize a man desirous to climb to the heaven of honour, kept under with the mountain of his prince's command; and yet had he arms and legs exempted from the suppression of that mountain. The word, *Tu mihi criminis author* (alluding to his prince's command): 'Thou art the occasion of my imputed cowardice.' His horse was trapped in the earthly strings of tree-roots, which, though their increase was stubbed down to the ground, yet were they not utterly deaded, but hoped for an after-resurrection. The word, *Spe alor*: 'I hope for a spring.' Upon his shield he bare a ball, stricken down with a man's hand that it might mount. The word, *Ferior ut efferar*: 'I suffer myself to be contemned because I will climb.'

The eighth had all his armour throughout engrailed like a crabbed briary hawthorn bush, out of which notwithstanding sprung (as a good child of an ill father) fragrant blossoms of delightful may flowers, that made, according to the nature of may, a most odoriferous smell. In the midst of this, his snowy curled top, round wrapped together, on the ascending of his crest, sat a solitary nightingale close encaged, with a thorn at her breast, having this mot in her mouth: *Luctus monumenta manebunt*. At the foot of this bush represented on his bases lay a number of black swollen toads gasping for wind, and summer-lived grasshoppers gaping after dew, both which were choked with excessive drought for want of shade. The word, *Non sine vulnere viresco*: 'I spring not without impediments', alluding to the toads and suchlike that erst lay sucking at his roots, but now were turned out and near choked with drought. His horse was suited in black and sandy earth, as adjacent to this bush, which was here and there patched with short burnt grass, and as thick ink-dropped with toiling ants and emmets as ever it might crawl, who, in the full of the summer moon (ruddy garnished on his horse's forehead) hoarded up their provision of grain against winter. The word, *Victrix fortunae sapientia*: 'Providence prevents misfortune.' On his shield he set forth the picture of death doing alms-deeds to a number of poor desolate children. The word, *Nemo alius explicat*: 'No other man takes pity upon us.' What his meaning was herein I cannot imagine, except death had done him and his brethren some great good turn in ridding them of some untoward parent or kinsman that would have been their confusion; for else I cannot see how death should have been said to do almsdeeds, except he had deprived them suddenly of their lives, to deliver them out of some further misery; which could not in any wise be, because they were yet living.

Thomas Nashe
The Unfortunate Traveller, 1594

The revival of interest in heraldry in Victorian times owed much to Sir Walter Scott, who regarded it as of great educational value.

What, is it possible? not know the figures of Heraldry? Of what could your father be thinking?

Sir Walter Scott
Rob Roy, 1817

'The skirts of the wood seem lined with archers, although only a few are advanced from its dark shadow.'
'Under what banner?' asked Ivanhoe.
'Under no ensign of war which I can observe,' answered Rebecca.

The Union Jack.

'A singular novelty,' muttered the knight, 'to advance to storm such a castle without pennon or banner displayed! – Seest thou who they be that act as leaders?'

'A knight, clad in sable armour, is the most conspicuous,' said the Jewess; 'he alone is armed from head to heel, and seems to assume the direction of all around him.'

'What device does he bear on his shield?' replied Ivanhoe.

'Something resembling a bar of iron, and a padlock painted blue on the black shield!'

'A fetterlock and shacklebolt azure,' said Ivanhoe. 'I know not who may bear the device, but well I ween it might now be mine own.'

Sir Walter Scott
Ivanhoe, 1819

The Union Jack

Why Union? Obviously because it unites three emblems of tutelar saints on one flag, and thereby denotes the union of three peoples under one Sovereign. It is the motto *Tria juncta in Uno* rendered in bunting.

Why Jack? Two theories are propounded, one fanciful, the other probable. Some say 'Jack' is the anglicized form of 'Jacques', which is the French signature of James I, in whose reign and by whose command the first Union Flag was called into being. Against this at least three reasons may justly be urged:

(1) The term *Jack* does not appear – so far as we can discover – in any warrant referring to the Jacobean Flag of 1606. It is rather in later documents that this term occurs.

(2) If the earliest Union Flag be a *Jack* just because it is the creation of James, then surely it follows that,

to be consistent, later Union Flags, the creations of later sovereigns, should have borne those Sovereigns' names; for example *The Union Anne*, *The Union George*!

(3) The English way of pronouncing 'Jacques' is not, and probably never was *Jack*, but *Jaikes*. The other, and more feasible theory, is as follows: The term 'Jaque' (e.g. *jaque de mailles*) was borrowed from the French and referred to any jacket or coat on which, especially, heraldic emblems were blazoned.

In days long prior to those of the first Stuart king, mention is made of 'whytte cotes with red crosses worn by shyppesmen and men of the cette of London', from which sentence we learn that the emblem of the nation's tutelar saint was (as in yet earlier Crusaders' days) a *fighter's* emblem. When such emblem or emblems were transferred to a flag, the term *Jaque* may well, in course of time, have been also applied to that flag, as previously to the jacket.

J. R. Crawford
'The Art of Heraldry' in Arthur Charles
Fox-Davies, *A Complete Guide to*
Heraldry, 1904

Visitations

Visitations were the tours of inspection made by heralds in England to survey and keep a record of the coats of arms and pedigrees of those using arms and to correct irregularities. They took place between 1530 and 1686 at intervals of about thirty years.

It was the duty of the Kings of Arms to survey and record the bearings and descent of the armigerous persons in their provinces and to correct arms irregularly used. In due course they began to devise arms for other persons of sufficient standing to bear them, and early in the 15th century they were definitely granting arms. At first their authority to do so was somewhat nebulous, but from early in the 16th century their patents of appointment have specifically conferred on them the power to grant arms.

Occasionally in the 15th century, and with some regularity in the following two centuries, the heralds made periodical circuits of various parts of the country, under the authority of Royal Commissions, to inquire into all matters connected with the bearing of arms, the use of styles of worship, to correct arms unlawfully borne or usurped, to collect information, and to draw up authoritative records. The Officer of Arms conducting a Visitation was empowered 'to put down or otherwise deface at his discretion' all unlawful arms, crests, cognizances, and devices, 'in plate, jewels, paper, parchment, windows, gravestones and monuments or elsewhere wheresoever they be set or placed'. He was also to make infamous by proclamation any person who unlawfully and without just authority had 'usurped and taken upon him any name or title of honour or dignity as esquire, gentleman or other'. A person summoned to appear before an Officer of Arms might satisfy him that the arms he bore were lawfully his, by grant to or ancient usage by an ancestor, or if he could not do this he might either have the arms rectified and recorded or he might disclaim all pretence and title thereto in the future.

There is evidence that some local visitations took place in the 15th century, but from 1530 they were held at intervals of about thirty years. The latest Commission of Visitations bears the date 13th May 1686. Most records compiled on these occasions are preserved at the College of Arms, and a large proportion of hereditary armorial bearings is borne on their authority.

Boutell's Heraldry, 1983

Visitation Commission, 1663

Charles the Second &c To our trusty and wellbeloved servant Sir *Edward Bishe* knight *Clarencieux* King of Armes of the south east and west parts of our realme of *England* from the river of *Trent* southwards and to all other our loving subjects greeting Forasmuch as God of his great clemency and goodness hath committed to our empire and goverance the nobility people and commons of this our realme of *England* and other our dominions wee mynding of our royall power and absolute authority to visitt survey and view throughout all our realme of *England* and other our dominions as well for a due order to be kept and observed in all things touching the office and dutyes appertaining to armes as alsoe for reformacion of diverse and sundry abuses and disorders daily arising and growing for want of ordinary visitacions surveys and views in tymes convenient according to the auncient forme and lawdable custome of the lawes of armes and that the nobility and gentry of this our realme may be preserved in every degree as appertayneth as well as in honour as in worshipp and that every person or persons bodyes politique corporate and others may be the better knowne in his or theire estate degree and mistery without confusion or disorder have therefore constituted deputed ordayned and appointed for us and in our name our said trusty and wellbeloved servant Sir *Edward Bish* k^t *Clarencieux* King of Arms of the south east and west parts of our realme of *England* from the said river of *Trent* southwards by himselfe or his sufficient deputy or deputyes under the seale of his office deputed and authorized to visitt all the said province and all *South Wales* and all the parts and members appertaining to the office and charge of the said *Clarencieux* King of Armes according to the lawes of armes from tyme to tyme as often and when as hee shall thinke most meet and convenient for the same and to convent and call before hym the said *Clarencieux* or his deputy or deputyes att such certayne places and convenient tymes as hee his deputy or deputyes shall appoint all manner of person or persons that doe or pretende to beare armes or are styled esquire or gentleman within all the aforesaid parts of our realme of *England* and *South Wales* and to cause all such persons then and there to produce and shewe forth by what authority and right they doe challenge and clayme the same And wee doe hereby further graunt unto our said servant and his deputy and deputyes full power lycence and authority…to enter upon reasonable request and att reasonable tymes in the day into all churches castells houses and other att his or their discrecion to peruse and take knowledge survey and view of all manner of armes cognizances crests and other devises of all and singular our subjects as well bodyes politic as others within all the aforesaid parts of our realme of *England* and *South Wales*.

The Patent Roll from the *Hastings Peerage Case* (1840), quoted in *Munimenta Heraldica*, 1484–1984

Shakespeare's coat of arms

The story of Shakespeare's coat of arms, detailed here in S. Schoenbaum's William Shakespeare: A Documentary Life *(1975), is an interesting example of the elaborate process required in the late 16th century to acquire this honour, and the problems it involved for the ordinary citizen.*

His father had made a preliminary approach to the Heralds' College, probably at some time after he became bailiff of Stratford in 1568, but then, as troubles closed in on him, let the matter drop. The heralds commanded heavy fees when the Shakespeares, beset by creditors, could ill afford them. Then, in 1596, John Shakespeare renewed his application – or, more likely, his son did so in his father's name. John was in his sixties, an old man for those days, and he would think twice before making the long and tiring journey by horse to London. On the other hand, William was there on the spot. If he started from scratch with a new application in his own name while his father still lived, the College of Arms would have regarded such a course as irregular: it was proper that the grant be made to the oldest male in the direct line, and to the member of the family who enjoyed the more dignified social position (former bailiffs rated more highly than playwrights). Yet there was nothing to prevent the eldest son from setting into motion the machinery for a grant in which the entire family would take pride.

Preserved at the College are two rough drafts of a document, dated 20 October 1596 and prepared by Sir William Dethick, Garter King of Arms, granting the request of John Shakespeare for a coat of arms. A note at the foot of one of these drafts describes 'This John' as having received a 'pattern' on paper 'under Clarent Cook's hand…xx years past'. That is how we know of the earlier application. The twenty years alluded to, carrying us back to 1576, may be taken as approximate. A 'pattern' was a trick, or pen-and-ink sketch, of a coat of arms. Robert Cook, then Clarenceux King of Arms, would for a fee have drawn it on paper, reserving parchment for the approved design. That stage was never reached when John first applied.

These heraldic documents often yield interesting genealogical details, but the 1596 draft grant is not in this respect especially communicative.… However, the note appended to the document furnishes a few supporting facts about the applicant himself – that 'xv or xvi years past' (a mistake for xxv and xxvi?) he was a justice of the peace and bailiff, and a Queen's officer; that he had 'lands and tenements of good wealth, and substance', worth £500; and that he had taken for his wife the daughter of a gentleman of worship. John Shakespeare was indeed the Queen's officer, for as bailiff he held the fortnightly Court of Record – a Crown court – and as coroner, almoner, and the like, also represented the Crown.

In consideration of these claims of honour, the Garter King of Arms declares that he has assigned and confirmed this shield: 'Gold, on a bend sables, a spear of the first steeled argent, and for his crest or cognizance a falcon, his wings displayed argent, standing on a wreath of his colours, supporting a spear gold, steeled as aforesaid, set upon a helmet with mantles and tassels as hath been accustomed and doth more plainly appear depicted on this margent.' In the upper left-hand corner of both drafts appears, as Garter indicates, a rough sketch of the trick of arms. At a time when heraldry tended towards fussiness and over-elaboration, the Shakespeare arms have a classic simplicity.

Above the shield and crest the clerk has written 'non, sanz droict'. The phrase gave him trouble. He scored it through, then repeated it, above, with initial capitals: 'Non, Sanz Droict'. At the head of the document he had a third go, this time putting the words in capitals and omitting the comma: 'NON SANZ DROICT'. Could the phrase conceivably signify an endorsement of heraldic correctness? Probably not – more likely it represents a motto, 'the invention or conceit of the bearer' (as one contemporary remarks); which required no *imprimatur* from the heralds. 'Non sanz droict' – *Not without right* – makes better sense than 'Non, Sanz Droict' – *No, without right*.… If [Shakespeare] did choose 'Non sanz droict' as his motto, neither he nor his descendants seem ever to have used it. No motto appears above the arms displayed in relief on the Shakespeare monument in Stratford church, nor was the phrase included on the gravestone of his daughter Susanna.…

The grant authorizes the Shakespeares to divide their shield vertically, with the Shakespeare bearings on the dexter half, and the Arden on the sinister.… But the heralds worried about the Ardens of Wilmcote (misspelt *Wellingcote* by the clerk). Did they trace their descent from the prestigious Ardens of Park Hall in Warwickshire? That would entitle them to 'Ermine, a fess checky gold and azure', a coat derived from the Beauchamps, Earls of Warwick. At first the heralds opted for this device, and sketched it impaled with the Shakespeare arms, then changed their minds, scratched it out, and alongside drew a differentiated form of the ancient Arden coat, 'Gules, three cross crosslets fitchées gold, and on a gold chief a martlet gules.' Evidently they felt, on second thought, that the Wilmcote Ardens rated only the less illustrious old coat. It has recently been suggested the latter may indicate a connection with the Cheshire and Staffordshire Ardens. In the end the Shakespeares decided not to impale their arms.…

The suppression of 'signs of feudalism'

In 1790 the French Revolution decided to suppress arms, together with 'signs of feudalism'. But until the fall of the royal family, an exception was made for 'interesting works of art', though it was revoked in autumn 1792. Throughout the following year a genuine 'heraldic terror' reigned vis-à-vis all moveable and immoveable property bearing arms, marks of nobility or monarchic emblems.

A bove: the arms of Paris in 1792. Opposite below: the Marshal of Noyes delays removing his arms from his Paris house.

1793, 12 October – Paris

Minutes of a meeting of the Committee on Arts and Monuments.

The Commune of Paris.
To the citizens.
Extract from the register of the minutes of the administrators of the Commission of Public Works, Arts and Monuments.

To citizen Avril,
the 18th *brumaire*
[second month of the French Republican calendar]
of the second year.
On the 21st day of the 1st month
of the second year
of the one and indivisible Republic.

'A member informed the assembly that there were plaques semy of fleurs-de-lis on the fireplaces of the Palais National des Thuileries and the Louvre.

He also noted that there were railings charged with signs of feudalism in copper and gilt bronze in the Menus Plaisirs.

The assembly, considering that a decree existed which enjoins that all signs of feudalism and all fleurs-de-lis must be removed, orders:

1. that the said fireplace plaques shall be turned over;

2. that the railings of the Menus Plaisirs shall be destroyed and authorizes the citizen controller of the Palais National to carry out these operations.

Citizen Avril then read out his petition on the cemeteries to be set up outside the large towns and on the monument of Les Invalides.

It was loudly applauded and the assembly decided to betake itself on the twenty-third day of the first month of the second year to the General Council,

Citizens call for the destruction of the arms in the Hôtel of Sancerre.

in order to read it to the Council and request the latter to support it before the National Convention.

Citizen Ameilhon informed the assembly that he had noticed, in various districts of Paris, signs of royalty and of feudalism and that these should be removed as soon as possible.

First he referred to an inscription from the reign of Louis XV, placed on the facing of the small Quai des Ormes.

Then to an infinite number of fleurs-de-lis scattered in all directions throughout the house of the *ci-devant* Célestins, it being of the utmost necessity to have removed those that covered the ceiling of a large hall used for the meetings of the *ci-devant* secretaries of the *ci-devant* king. They were painted in gold on an Azure background. He called for this ceiling to be covered with a coat of white or yellow; he added that, within this same monument, there were three belfries bearing fleuretty crosses; stained-glass

windows charged with fleurs-de-lis were situated both in the Chapel of the Blind and in the church and one of the halls.

He also declared that, in the Rue des Roziers, in the Marais, beside a large carriage gateway, at no. 37, there was a stone bearing an inscription in Gothic letters beginning with these words: here begins the fief of Loys, etc.

He concluded by saying that Rue de Grenelle, in the suburb of St Germain, on the church of St Chaumont and on those of the *ci-devant* Carmelites, several crosses were charged with clearly visible fleurs-de-lis.

One of the members observed that they should have been removed.

A member informed the assembly that the police-court magistrate of the Arsenal section had called for the walls of the court where he presided to be covered with Republican paper in place of that which had to be removed.

On hearing this request, the assembly moved on to the agenda, on the grounds that the request did not concern it and referred the police-court magistrate of the said section to take the matter before the relevant authority.'
Signed: Avril, administrator of public works and president. Coulombeau, clerk secretary. Certified a true extract, Coulombeau, clerk secretary.
(Extract from the register of the minutes of the Commission, Archives nationales, Paris, after Rémi Mathieu, *Le système héraldique français*, 1946)

The Japanese *mon*

Among the various systems of emblems used in non-western societies, the one that is most disconcertingly close to European heraldry is to be found in traditional Japan. Moreover, as in the West, in the course of the 12th century these emblems, which until then had been purely individual, became dynastic and hereditary. However, there are also marked differences between European arms and the Japanese mon.

Japanese heraldic art is marked by its great flexibility and total freedom of expression; it is imbued with a charming fantasy and the charges used take on the most diverse forms, sometimes combined in an altogether unexpected manner. Since the artist was not restricted by any code or 'grammar', he could give free rein to his imagination. Yet the design was based on a rigorous geometrical balance and always remained loyal to a formal stylistic tradition. It also has its own terminology, to designate not only the charges and their position, but also their construction. Generally circular, the shield or *mon* can also take the form of a square, a rectangle, a lozenge or a hexagon reminiscent of the scales of a tortoise, modified by the incurvation of the edges or the rounding off of the corners. In some cases, especially when the arms are intended as decoration on a fabric, the border line is suppressed. Like the western heraldists before the 16th century, the Japanese heraldists feared empty space and made sure that the charges filled the shield and followed its shape. This meant that a cluster of wisteria blossom, a crane in flight or a butterfly drawn according to this principle would still follow a circular design; inspection of one of the shields of the Ghelre armorial (14th century) would show much the same; the lion or the eagle charged on it retain the triangular form of the mould.

Japanese heraldry does not use lines of partition; the design of most arms is simple, comprising only one charge, sometimes two or three, rarely more. Yet it is not uncommon to find the arms of different families associated on the same *mon* as a result of grants of arms or marriages. Moreover, although there are no clan arms as such in Japan, as there are in Scotland or Poland, the influence of certain major families is reflected in the arms of their vassals, based either on similitude or augmentations; this has made it possible to classify arms by region.

The charges stand out in gold against a black background, like Chinese lacquer designs; sometimes vice versa. The colours, which are rarely used, are dark blue, light blue, red, brown and green. They are employed rather to stress the contours than applied in flat tints; on the other hand, they stand out brightly on the banners alongside white and yellow.

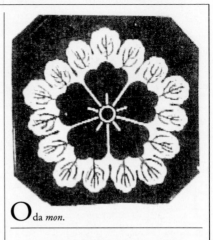

O da *mon*.

The charges

The charges are many and varied; but they include few geometrical forms analogous to those we describe as 'ordinaries'. The horizontal and vertical bands we blazon as the 'fess' and the 'pale' simply express, depending on how many there are, the numbers 'one' (*hitotsu*), 'two' (*futatsu*) or 'three' (*mitsu*). The cross has the same origin, deriving from the ideogram for the number 'ten' (*tō*). What is most extraordinary is that this last number, modified in various ways, has produced a whole variety of crosses that could be thought of as western: rounded, couped, saltire couped, potent, cross-crosslet, etc., so that when St François Xavier arrived in Japan he could not at first understand why the emblem of our faith appeared on the arms of many non-Christian families....

While the *monchō* of the military nobility can be recognized by the martial attributes, that of the noble courtiers is characterized by flowers, plants, insects and small animals.

The six-petalled chrysanthemum or *kiku* is the emblem of the empire; that of the imperial family is the graceful *kiri* or Paulownia flower, with its three thyrses bearing five, seven and nine buds.

The emperors granted these arms to a number of daimyos as a reward for exceptional services rendered, just as the kings of France used to grant the fleur-de-lis for the same reason. Thus Ashikaga Takauji, powerful vassal of the shogun, was granted the privilege of bearing the *kiri* on his arms by Emperor Godaigo as a reward for supporting him in 1333.

Anyone who leafs through a Japanese armorial such as the *Heian Monkan* (1953) would feel as though they were wandering through an enchanted garden; there is a proliferation of flowers and plants of all kinds, designed in a highly sophisticated manner: budding, flowering, shown in profile or reversed. There are wisteria (*fuji*), with coiled or spiralling clusters of blossoms, cherry blossoms (*sakura*), plum blossoms (*ume*), peonies (*botan*), carnations (*nadeshiko*), gentians (*rindō*), irises (*kakitsubata*), mistletoe (*hoya*), tea flower capsules (*chanomi*), little orange

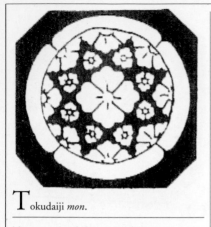

Tokudaiji *mon*.

blossoms (*tachibana*), trefoils
(*katabami*), mallow leaves (*aoi*), ivy
(*tsuta*), bamboo (*sasa*), cloves of garlic
(*chōji*), ginger (*myōga*), hemp (*asa*), rice
(*ine* or, when it is in sheaves, *abane-ine*),
mulberry (*kuwanoki*), cedar (*sugi*),
maple (*kaédé-momiji*) and palm
trees (*shuro*).

The lion (*shishi*) found so commonly
in European heraldry is rare here; its
strange design shows that it was in fact
unknown in Japan. The horse (*uma*)
is always shown without saddle or
halter.... The dog (*inu*), the goat, the
hind (*shika*), the monkey (*saru*) and the
boar (*inoshishi*) are uncommon. Among
small animals, the rabbit (*usagi*) is
definitely the favourite in *monchō*
(blazon); it is shown facing the
spectator, in profile, sitting or very often
running to avoid a wave about to engulf
it. When more than one is depicted, it is
usually in the form of two rabbits
'affronty' or three arranged 'in pairle',
with their little bottoms joined. The rat
(*ne*), tortoise (*kame*) and bat (*kōmori*)
also occur in Japanese heraldry.

The heads and limbs of the animals
are never cut off or torn off as in
European·heraldry. The stag can be
shown with antlers, but they are separate
from its forehead and affronty, described
as *dakizuno* ('embraced horns').

Among birds, we find the crane
(*tsuru*), the wild duck (*karigane*) whose
design is reminiscent of the martlet, the
dove (*hato*), the sparrow (*suzume*) and
the cock (*niwatori*). The main insects
are the butterfly (*chō*) and the dragonfly
(*tombo*). The butterfly, when shown
sitting with its wings spread, is blazoned
yoroichō; in profile and in flight it is
described as *agehanochō*.

I shall conclude this list of the
Japanese bestiary with the denizens of
the deep: fish (*sakana*), the crayfish
(*ebi*), the scallop (*ichi-itaya*), a kind of
harp shell seen from below (*sazae*) and
the clam (*hamaguri*).

A living heraldry

I discovered the extent to which heraldic
art is flourishing in Japan during a visit
there: up-dated armorials are frequently
published and there are heraldic artists
who make a living from their art, having
formed themselves into trade
associations in the large towns,
particularly in Tokyo, Kyoto, Nagoya
and Osaka.

In Kyoto a specialist library put me
in touch with a professional heraldist,
Mr Chiyoso Hirose, President of the
Association of Heraldic Arts and Vice-
President of the General Association of
Japanese Heraldry, the federation of the
associations.

The corporation to which he belongs
produces heraldic designs intended for a
variety of uses, among which it is worth
noting the creation of armorials such
as the *Heian Monkan* ('Mirror of the
Heian Arms'). He was responsible for
publishing it in Kyoto in 1953. But a
large part of his work is devoted to

designing stencils, widely used for decorating silk and cotton fabrics. Before acquiring the necessary technical expertise and perfect mastery of the subject, heraldic artists have to undergo a five or six-year apprenticeship. The stencils are created by using a special paper coated with *perilla ocimoides* and *shibu* oil, which is obtained from the green persimmon fruit. They are cut out with a burin and require both patience and skill on the part of the artist.

In a Japan seething with the fever of progress in the political, economic, scientific and technical fields, heraldry thus continues to flourish, while also adapting to the conditions of our times.

Early this century, H. G. Ströhl, in the introduction to his magisterial study *Japanisches Wappenbuch, 'Nihon Moncho'*, declared that only personal arms existed in Japan and that arms of towns or corporations were unknown there. And that was true. Since then this gap has been filled: the *Heian Monkan* (1953) referred to above contains the arms of 149 towns. They look ultra-modern; the wind of abstraction has withered the few, rare flowers to be found in it. Only the gentian, an attribute of the Minamoto shoguns in Kamakura, retains the freshness of earlier times; the butterflies, sparrows, wild ducks and cranes have fled; a bank of sand emerges in Sumoto; in Hamamatsu an ancient star sparkles above a circular spray of water, but there is no rabbit to be seen. Instead, a crowd of western five or-six pointed stars light up the scene. Geometry has won the day and engendered all the new symbols. The arms of Tokyo, the capital, consists of a circle furnished with six teeth and containing a little disc; Kyoto, the town of the temples, palaces and enchanted gardens, was also endowed with a circle

with three points and three teeth. These would appear to be erudite amalgams of the ideograms forming their names.

The volume in question does not contain the arms of corporations; yet they do exist and can be seen borne on the backs of their members, such as the three arrows of the association of hawkers. To this category, a new one has been added, the *mon* of tradesmen; these are in fact marks and not arms, however they have still been accepted in the *Hyōjun Monchō* ('Armorial designs') published in Tokyo in 1958, after the arms of important families and of towns. The large stores, large hotels and representatives of European firms appear there and, surprisingly, we even find the dog listening to his master's voice proudly encircled in a *mon*.

These are of course merely advertisements that cannot do any harm to heraldry and in fact simply demonstrate the popularity it has achieved. The *Nihon no monchō* is an ancient tree whose roots reach down to the history of the Middle Ages and whose inexhaustible sap still keeps the foliage green and produces new shoots from the trunk, in the shade of the kiri flowers wreathed round its crown.

René le Juge de Segrais,
'L'héraldique japonaise'
in the catalogue of the exhibition
Emblèmes, totems, blasons,
Musée Guimet, March–June 1964

The words to say it

The language used in English heraldry today dates back to Norman French and might therefore seem difficult for the layman to understand. However, contrary to general belief, it is neither esoteric nor inaccessible. A few hours' effort would suffice to learn the hundred odd words and basic grammar of blazon needed to describe more than eighty per cent of armorial bearings.

Abatement: term for certain armorial symbols or charges that were marks of dishonour in some countries

A rgent a Bend Gules between six Cross crosslets fitchy Azure

Achievement: a full display of armorial bearings

Addorsed: describes two charges, generally identical, shown back to back

Affronty: describes charges, generally animals, shown with head and body facing the spectator

Alerion: a small eagle displayed without beak or legs

Annulet: 1. a ring 2. cadency mark of

A zure a Bend Or charged in Chief with an Annulet Sable

the fifth son in English heraldry

Argent: the tincture silver/white

Armed: 1. describes any beast or bird of prey having teeth, talons, horns or claws of a different tincture from the body 2. wearing armour

Armiger: a person entitled to bear heraldic arms

Armorial: collection of armorial bearings, painted or blazoned

Azure: the heraldic tincture blue

Bar: diminutive of a fess

Barruly or **Burely:** a barry field of ten or more divisions

Barry: describes a shield or charges divided horizontally into an even number of equal parts of alternate tinctures

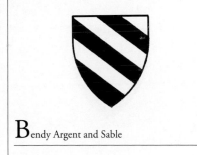

Bendy Argent and Sable

broad band descending from the dexter chief to the sinister base to divide the shield into two equal parts on either side

Bend sinister: an ordinary in the form of a broad band descending from the sinister chief to the dexter base to divide the shield into two equal parts on either side

Bendy: describes a shield or charge divided by bends into an even number of equal parts of alternate tinctures

Between: describes the main charge

Argent a Bend Sable

Base: in England, the bottom part of a shield, not more than a third or less than a fifth

Basilisk or **Cockatrice:** fabulous animal, generally represented by a dragon with the head of a cock

Baton: a couped bendlet

Beaked: describes a bird whose beak has a different tincture from the body

Bend: an ordinary in the form of a

Or semy of ten Billets Gules 4, 3, 2, 1

of a shield when secondary ones appear on either side

Bezant or **Besant:** small circular charge, always gold in England

Argent a Bordure Sable

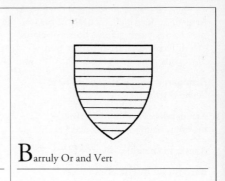

Barruly Or and Vert

Bezanty: semy of bezants

Billet: a small rectangular, geometrical charge, generally placed vertically

Billetty: semy of billets

Blazon: technical language for the written description of armorial bearings

Paly Argent and Azure over all a Bend Gules

Bordure: a border or band running round, and touching the edge of, the shield

Bretessed: embattled counterembattled when the inward and outward embattlements lie opposite each other

Buckle: stylized charge in the form of a buckle

Canting arms: a coat of arms where the charge is a pun on the owner's name

Canton: a sub-ordinary consisting of a

Or a Cross pommy Azure between four plain Crosses Gules

small square in the dexter chief of the shield unless otherwise blazoned

Charge: generic term for pictorial

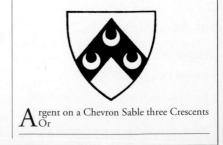

Argent on a Chevron Sable three Crescents Or

representations that can be placed on various parts of the shield (animals, plants, objects, etc.), as opposed to ordinaries and lines of partition,

Azure on a Saltire Argent a Crescent Gules in centre point

Argent a Chief Sable

which have a fixed place

Checky or **Chequy:** a pattern formed by horizontal and vertical lines intersecting

Vert a fess Or between two Chevrons Argent

at right angles and forming a kind of chessboard of alternate tinctures

Chevron: an ordinary in the form of an inverted V, the point usually directed towards the centre of the chief

Chevronny: describes a shield and its charges divided into an even number of equal chevrons of alternate tinctures

Chief: the upper part of a shield, not more than a third or less than a fifth

Cinquefoil: stylized flower with five radiating petals or leaves

Colour: generic term which in blazon refers only to Gules, Sable, Azure, Vert and Purpure (that is, not the metals or furs)

Compony or **Gobony:** describes ordinaries divided into equal square or rectangular compartments of alternate tinctures

Contourné: describes an animal where both the body and head face to the sinister

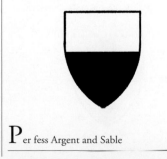

Per fess Argent and Sable

Barruly (or Burely) Argent and Azure over all a Lion rampant Gules crowned Or

Coronet: a support for a crest that is shaped like a crown. Five different coronets of rank may surmount the arms of English peers

Or three Escallops Azure

Cotise: originally a diminutive of the bend and depicted on either side of it, but any ordinary may now be cotised

Or a Cross Sable

Quarterly per fess indented Argent and Gules in dexter chief a Mullet Sable

Couchant: a beast lying down on all fours with its head raised

Couped: cut with a straight edge in contrast to erased, which has a jagged edge. It can be used both for a charge, such as a lion's head, and for an ordinary that terminates before reaching the edge of the shield

Crest: the generic term for the

Quarterly, 1 and 4: Sable a Cross engrailed Argent; 2 and 3: Or a Cross moline Gules

Per saltire Or and Sable

ornaments mounted on helmets

Cross-crosslet: describes a cross, each arm of which is crossed

Chequy Or and Sable

Crowned: animals wearing a crown

Dancetty or **Dancetté:** line of partition composed of deep indentations

Dexter: describes the right-hand side of the shield (left for the spectator)

Difference, mark of: a charge added to arms to indicate cadency

Dimidiation: method of impalement in which the dexter half of one coat of arms was joined to the sinister half of the other

Azure semy of Cross crosslets fitchy two Lucies haurient addorsed Or a Bordure engrailed Argent

Double-headed: having two heads, often describing the eagle

Embattled: describes an ordinary or line of partition whose upper edge is crenellated

Embattlement: with an indented edge

Argent two bars Sable

looking like battlements

Embowed: describes charges with curved or bent edges

Barry Argent and Sable

Engrailed: describes scalloped ordinaries and lines of partition, the points of the scalloping pointing outwards

Erased: cut with a jagged edge

Ermine: fur represented in stylized manner by black 'tails' on a white field

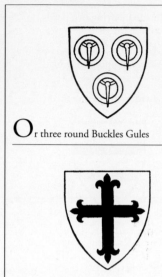

Or three round Buckles Gules

Or a Cross flory Sable

Escutcheon: small charge in the form of a shield

Fess: ordinary in the form of a broad horizontal band across the centre of the shield occupying not more than one third or less than one fifth of the shield

Fess point: the exact centre of the shield

Checky Or and Azure on a Canton Argent a Lion rampant Gules

Field: the surface of a shield on which charges are placed

Fitchy, **Fitché** or **Fitched:** pointed at the foot

Floretty: a charge, usually a cross, with fleur-de-lis sprouting from its arms

Argent fretty Sable

Flory or **Fleury:** charges terminating in fleur-de-lis

Sable a Lion rampant queue fourché Or

Fretty: a pattern of interlaced bendlets and bendlets sinister resembling a trellis

Furs: tinctures representing in a conventional and stylized manner the pelts with which combatants sometimes covered their shields in the 12th and 13th centuries. The two main furs are Vair and Ermine

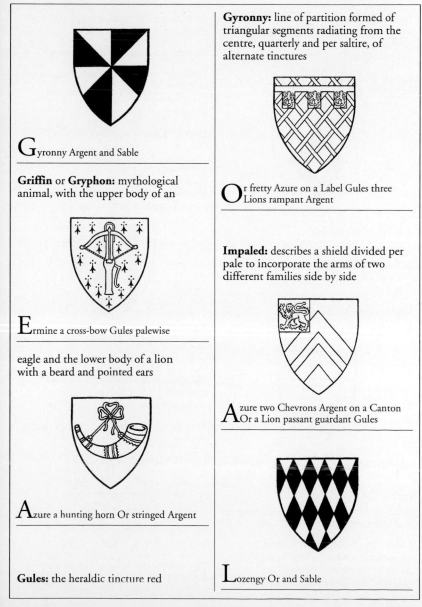

Gyronny: line of partition formed of triangular segments radiating from the centre, quarterly and per saltire, of alternate tinctures

Gyronny Argent and Sable

Griffin or **Gryphon:** mythological animal, with the upper body of an

Ermine a cross-bow Gules palewise

eagle and the lower body of a lion with a beard and pointed ears

Azure a hunting horn Or stringed Argent

Gules: the heraldic tincture red

Or fretty Azure on a Label Gules three Lions rampant Argent

Impaled: describes a shield divided per pale to incorporate the arms of two different families side by side

Azure two Chevrons Argent on a Canton Or a Lion passant guardant Gules

Lozengy Or and Sable

Issuant or **Jessant:** describes a charge emerging from an ordinary, a line of partition, another charge or the border of the shield

Label: small charge depicted by a horizontal band from which depend a number of rectangular or trapezoid

Argent a Mascle Sable

ordinaries. In England it is the cadency mark of an eldest son in the lifetime of his father

Lambrequin see **Mantling**

Langued: describes quadrupeds and

Argent a Fess Azure between six Martlets Gules

more generally the lion when the tongue is a different tincture from the rest

Lines of partition: generic term for geometrical shapes formed by lines of partition (vertical, horizontal or diagonal) that divide the shield into an

even number of equal parts of alternate tinctures

Lozenge: a diamond-shaped charge

Lozengy: describes a shield with charges and lines of partition divided into equal-sized lozenges of alternate tinctures by a number of criss-cross lines

Luce or **Lucy:** elongated, stylized pike-like fish

Mantling: an ornament separate from the shield in the form of flowing drapery attached to the helmet, often scalloped or with jagged edges

Paly undy Argent and Sable

Martlet: small charge in the form of a stylized bird, shown in profile and without feet or claws

Mascle: small geometrical charge in the form of a voided lozenge

Barruly Or and Azure an Orle of Martlets Gules

Mill rind or **Fer-de-moline:** the iron centrepiece of a millstone; a stylized charge formed of two C-shaped hooks

Argent a pall Sable

addorsed, sometimes attached by a small horizontal cross-bar

Molet or **Mullet:** small geometrical charge in the form of a star, generally with five points, sometimes pierced with a hole

Or a pale Sable

Paly Azure and Or on a Bend Gules a Crown between two Eagles displayed Argent

Mount: stylized charge in a crest depicting a mound

Per pale dexter Gules a Lion rampant Argent crowned Or *sinister* Argent an Orle Vert

Naissant: describes a charge that issues from the middle of another charge. It is seldom used in English heraldry

Or: the heraldic tincture gold, sometimes depicted as yellow

Ordinaries: generic term for geometric charges obtained by the division of the shield by horizontal, vertical or diagonal lines

Orle: a narrow border parallel, but not touching, the edge of the shield

Over all: describes a charge superimposed on other charges

Pale: a charge in the form of a broad vertical band in the centre of the shield

Pall: a Y-shaped charge rising from the base point of the shield towards the two corners of the chief

Paly: describes a shield, ordinaries, lines of partition and any charges divided vertically into an even number of equal parts of alternate tinctures

Passant: describes quadrupeds shown horizontally, in profile and walking

Paty: describes a cross or saltire whose arms widen at the end

Per fess: describes a shield or charge divided horizontally into two even parts

A zure on a Bend Or three Cinquefoils Sable *impaling* Argent two Bars Gules

Pile: an ordinary consisting of a wedge placed per pale, normally issuing from the top of the shield and converging in the base. It may also issue from the side

S able three chess rooks Argent

Plate: small circular charge, always silver in England

Point: term for the base of the shield

Potent: crutch-shaped. 1. a variety of the armorial fur Vair; 2. a Cross potent has crutch-shaped limbs

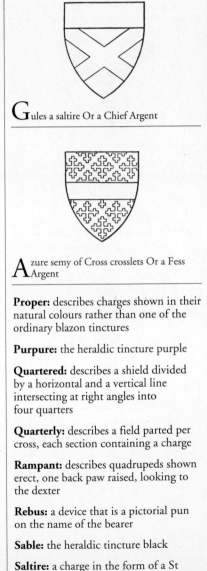

G ules a saltire Or a Chief Argent

A zure semy of Cross crosslets Or a Fess Argent

Proper: describes charges shown in their natural colours rather than one of the ordinary blazon tinctures

Purpure: the heraldic tincture purple

Quartered: describes a shield divided by a horizontal and a vertical line intersecting at right angles into four quarters

Quarterly: describes a field parted per cross, each section containing a charge

Rampant: describes quadrupeds shown erect, one back paw raised, looking to the dexter

Rebus: a device that is a pictorial pun on the name of the bearer

Sable: the heraldic tincture black

Saltire: a charge in the form of a St

Per bend Argent and Sable

Andrew's cross

Semy or **Semé:** describes a shield, an ordinary or any charge strewn with an indeterminate number of small charges

Shield: area demarcated by a border of

Vair

(Vair and Ermine)

Torteau: a red roundel. In French blazon, any roundel that is neither Or nor Argent

Undy: describes ordinaries and lines of

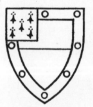

Per fess Argent and Azure a Border Vert bezanty and over all a Canton Ermine

varying shapes on which arms are placed

Sinister: designates the left-hand side of the shield (right for the spectator)

Supporters: term for the figures around the shield and appearing to support it. In French heraldry, some theorists distinguish between human supporters (*tenants*), beasts (*supports*) and inanimate objects or plants (*soutiens*)

Tincture: generic term for the heraldic metals (Or and Argent), colours (Gules, Sable, Azure, Vert, Purpure) and furs

Argent a fess dancetty Sable

partition with slightly wavy bordure lines

Vair: fur represented by alternate white and blue bell-shaped pieces, arranged in horizontal rows

Vairy: term used for Vair when it is not coloured white and blue

Vert: the heraldic tincture green (French: *sinople*)

Glossary adapted from
Michel Pastoureau, *Traité d'héraldique*
1993

FURTHER READING

INTRODUCTIONS AND MANUALS

Boutell, Charles, *Boutell's Heraldry*, 1983
Dennys, Rodney, *The Heraldic Imagination*, 1975
—, *Heraldry and the Heralds*, 1982
Fox-Davies, Arthur Charles, *A Complete Guide to Heraldry*, 1969
—, *The Book of Public Arms*, 1915
Friar, Stephen, *Heraldry*, 1992
—, and John Ferguson, *Basic Heraldry*, 1993
Grant, Francis J., *The Manual of Heraldry*, 1937
Hope, William Henry St John, *A Grammar of English Heraldry*, 1953
Marks, Richard, and Ann Payne (eds.), *British Heraldry from its Origins to c. 1800*, 1978
Moncreiffe, Iain, and Don Pottinger, *Simple Heraldry, Cheerfully Illustrated*, 1963
Neubecker, Ottfried, *Heraldry: Sources, Symbols and Meaning*, trans. Nicholas Fry, 1976
Puttock, Arthur Geoffrey, *A Dictionary of Heraldry and Related Subjects*, 1971
Rowland-Entwhistle, Theodore, *Heraldry*, 1984
Saffroy, Gaston and G. Saffroy, *Bibliographie généalogique, héraldique et nobiliaire de la France*, 1968–90
Wagner, Anthony R., *English Genealogy*, 1972
—, *Heraldry in England*, 1946
—, *Heralds and Ancestors*, 1978
—, *Heralds of England: A History of the Office and College of Arms*, 1967
Woodcock, Thomas, and John Martin Robinson, *The Oxford Guide to Heraldry*, 1988
Wright, Cyril Ernest, *English Heraldic Manuscripts in the British Museum*, 1973

MEDIEVAL HERALDRY

Brault, Gerard J., *Early Blazon. Heraldic Terminology in the 12th and 13th Centuries*, 1972
Pastoureau, Michel, *Les Armoiries*, 1976
—, *L'Hermine et le Sinople. Etudes d'héraldique médiévale*, 1979
Wagner, Anthony R., *A Catalogue of British Medieval Rolls of Arms*, 1950
—, *Heralds and Heraldry in the Middle Ages*, 1956
Young, Noël Denholm, *History and Heraldry, 1254 to 1310. A Study of the Historical Value of the Rolls of Arms*, 1965

THE RULES AND TERMINOLOGY OF HERALDRY

Elvin, Charles Norton, *A Dictionary of Heraldry*, 1889
Gough, Henry, *A Glossary of Terms used in Heraldry*, 1894

DE Montaigne

LIST OF ILLUSTRATIONS

The following abbreviations have been used:
a above; *b* below; *c* centre; *l* left; *r* right; AN
Archives Nationales, Paris; BN Bibliothèque
Nationale, Paris.

COVER

Front Arms of the vassals of both the Archbishop
of Trier and the Archbishop of Cologne. Bellenville
Armorial, c. 1380. BN
Spine Corporate arms in the *Armorial général*, 1696
Back a English armorial, 16th century. College of
Arms, London
Back b Limit of the City of London

OPENING

1 King Charles VII of France. In the *Grand Armorial
équestre de la Toison d'or*, copied and painted c.
1435–40. BN
2 Jean de Créquy. Ibid.
3 The Archbishop of Rheims. Ibid.
4 The King of Poland. Ibid.
5 Guy de Pontalier. Ibid.
6 The Duke of Brittany. Ibid.
7 Tibaud de Neufchâtel. Ibid.
8 Philippe de Ternant. Ibid.
9 Charles the Bold, Count of Charolais. Ibid.
11 Embarking on the Crusades. French manuscript,
14th century

CHAPTER 1

12 Hartmann von Aue. Miniature, c. 1300–10,
from *Manesse Codex*. University Library, Heidelberg
13 Hugolin de Schoenegg, Marshal of the papal
duchy of Spoleto, Basel. St Leonard's Church, Basel.
Historisches Museum, Basel
14 and 15 Rich butchers from the Nuremberg
carnival. Miniatures, late 15th century. Bodleian
Library, Oxford
16 Ivory chesspiece (rook or castle) from the treasury
of the Abbey of St Denis, late 11th century. BN
17 Greek vase depicting Hercules fighting three
warriors, 4th century BC. BN
18 Enamel plaque from the tomb of Geoffrey
Plantagenet, Count of Anjou, formerly in Le Mans
Cathedral, c. 1155–60. Musée Tessé, Le Mans
19l Combat between a Norman knight and a Saxon
footsoldier. Bayeux tapestry (tapestry of Queen
Matilda), late 11th century. Musée de la Tapisserie de
Bayeux, Bayeux
19r William the Conqueror raising his visor. Bayeux
tapestry (tapestry of Queen Matilda), late 11th
century. Musée de la Tapisserie de Bayeux, Bayeux

20a Seal of Amaury VII, Viscount of Thouars, 1223.
AN
20c Seal of Prince Louis of France, 1211. AN
20b Seal of Ingolf du Manoir, Norman peasant,
1247. AN
21a Charter sealed with the seal of the city of
Damme (1371). Municipal archives, Lübeck.
21b Seal of Eleanor of Castile, wife of Edward I,
1254. AN
22 The Lady Chapel, Bristol Cathedral
23a Stained-glass window in Bere Regis Church,
Dorset
23bl English stained-glass window, c. 1500
23br Jean du Mez, Marshal of France, receiving the
oriflamme, c. 1220–5. Chartres Cathedral
24a Swiss wooden coffer covered with painted
parchment, early 14th century. Schweizerisches
Landesmuseum, Zurich
24b Tomb of Philippe Pot, Great Chamberlain of
Louis XI and Seneschal of Burgundy, late 15th
century. Louvre, Paris
25 The Count and Countess of Salisbury in full
heraldic dress. Miniature, c. 1483–5. British Library,
London.
26–7 Review of helmets in the cloister. Painting from
the *Livre des tournois* of King René, c. 1460. BN
28–9 How the jousters fight in herds. Painting from
the *Livre des tournois* of King René, c. 1460. BN
30c Majolica plate with the arms of Pope Julius II, c.
1510–5. Metropolitan Museum of Art, New York
30b The arms of Death. Woodcut by Albrecht Dürer,
1503. Cabinet des Estampes, BN
31 Emblems of the various guilds in Orvieto, 1602.
Museo dell'Opera del Duomo, Orvieto
32–3 Portuguese planisphere by Teixera showing the
world divided between Spaniards and Portuguese,
1573. BN
34–5a Part of the royal edict from the *Armorial
général*, 1696. AN
34b Bookbinding with the first arms of Jacques-
Auguste de Thou, c. 1582. Réserve des Imprimés,
BN
35 Arms of Parisian corporations in the *Armorial
général*, 1696. BN
36a Device of the French republic and revolutionary
emblems. Coloured print, 1794
36b Viscount Mathieu de Montmorency. Lithograph
by Caminade, c. 1820. BN
37c Louis XVI in his coronation robes. Painting by
Joseph-Siffrein Duplessis, 1778. Musée Carnavalet,
Paris
37b Report by the Inspector of Highways, Monsieur
Chaillou, on the undestroyed arms in the Rue Neuve
des Petits Champs, 28 November 1790. AN
38l The eagle chosen by Napoleon Bonaparte as the
emblem of his empire. BN

DOCUMENTS

INDEX

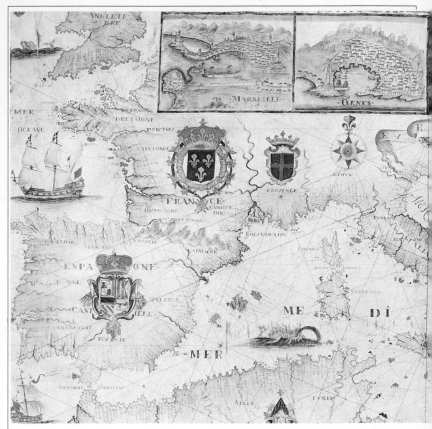

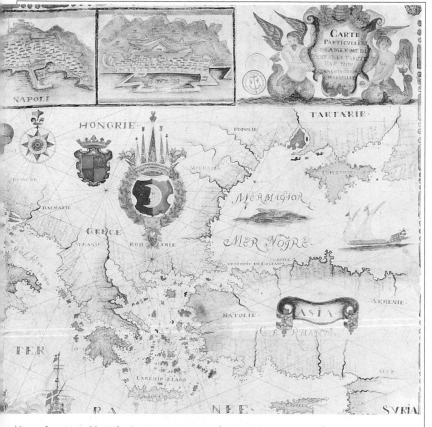

ACKNOWLEDGMENTS

The publisher thanks Thomas Woodcock, Somerset Herald, for his invaluable advice on the main text.

PHOTO CREDITS

TEXT CREDITS

S. Schoenbaum, *William Shakespeare. A Documentary Life*, Oxford University Press, 1975; reprinted by permission of Oxford University Press.

Michel Pastoureau
was born in 1947. He is an archivist, paleographer
and director of studies at the Ecole Pratique des
Hautes Etudes, where he has held a chair in the
history of western symbolism since 1983.
His early work was on the history of emblems and
related fields (heraldry, the study of seals and coins).
His current research focuses on the history of colours
and relations between humans and animals.
Michel Pastoureau has written about thirty books.
His most recent publications are: *Couleurs, images,
symboles* (1989), *L'Echiquier de Charlemagne* (1990),
Dictionnaire des couleurs de notre temps (1992),
Traité d'héraldique (1993) and *Une histoire
des rayures et des tissus rayés* (1995). He is
a member of the International Academy of
Heraldry and Vice-President of the
French heraldry society, the Société
Française d'Héraldique.

Translated from the French by Francisca Garvie

First published in the United Kingdom in 1997 by
Thames & Hudson Ltd,
181A High Holborn, London WC1V 7QX

Reprinted 2001, 2004

English translation © 1997
Thames and Hudson Ltd, London

© 1996 Gallimard

British Library Cataloguing-in-Publication Data

A catalogue record for this book is available
from the British Library

ISBN 0–500–30074–7

Printed and bound in Italy
by Editoriale Lloyd, Trieste